RETURN TO WINESBURG

*The University
of
North Carolina
Press*

Chapel Hill

Sherwood Anderson

Selections from Four Years of Writing for a Country Newspaper

RETURN TO
WINESBURG

Edited with an Introduction by
RAY LEWIS WHITE

In Honor Of

MAXWELL GEISMAR

ACKNOWLEDGMENTS

I am happy to thank the following persons for addressing their good will and their professional skills toward the publication of this book: Mrs. Robert Lane Anderson; Mr. Samuel M. Boone, The University of North Carolina Library; Mrs. Amy Nyholm, Manuscripts Curator, The Newberry Library; Mr. Joe Stephenson; Mr. James Tindall; Mr. Lawrence W. Towner, Director and Librarian, The Newberry Library; Mr. Ivan von Auw, Harold Ober Associates, Incorporated; and Mr. James M. Wells, Associate Director, The Newberry Library, who graciously allowed me to reprint selected material from The Newberry Library Bulletin, *of which he is editor.*

More personally, I am grateful to Mr. Maxwell Geismar for advising me on editorial procedures and to Mrs. Sherwood Anderson for her continuing friendship and her encouragement of my work.

RLW

CONTENTS

1927

1928

1929

Contents   [xi]

ILLUSTRATIONS

RETURN TO WINESBURG

The people of Winesburg, Ohio, perform a curious dance of life. Always lonely and usually inarticulate, they once or perhaps twice in their lifetimes come close to true communication with each other. These men and women are Sherwood Anderson's "grotesques." Warped psychically and often physically, never able to sustain more than momentary entrance into another's tortured existence, each haltingly approaches another's suffering and then recoils to suffer alone. There is Alice Hindman, unable to let anyone touch even her bedroom furniture because it is her own. Kate Swift, stern and cold toward her students, cries alone at night, for she is in reality the most passionate soul in Winesburg. The Reverend Curtis Hartman, watching Kate through the cracked stained-glass window of his church, makes of the crying woman a messenger of God. And Doctor Parcival, not wanting the sick to come to him for healing, knows that "everyone in the world is Christ and they are all crucified." [1]

Yet these grotesque men and women have a strange beauty. Their unrelieved suffering is "delicious, like the twisted little apples that grow in the orchards of Winesburg. In the fall one walks in the orchards and the ground is hard with frost underfoot. . . . On the trees are only a few gnarled apples that the pickers have rejected. . . . One nibbles at them and they are delicious. Into a little round place at the side of the apple has been gathered all of its sweetness. One runs from tree to tree over the frosted ground picking the gnarled, twisted apples and filling his pockets with them. Only the few know the sweetness of the twisted apples." [2]

The pattern of Sherwood Anderson's own life demonstrates his recognition of both the agony and the beauty of small-town life. George Willard, the central figure of *Winesburg, Ohio,* is a young newspaper reporter who knows or hears most of the stories of Winesburg's unhappy lives. He decides to escape from the town, to become a "successful" man in the great unnamed city for which he departs. And Sherwood Anderson, having achieved literary and social success after the publication of *Winesburg, Ohio* in 1919, decided in 1927 "to return to Winesburg"—to live in Marion, Virginia, and, like George Willard, to be a small-town newspaperman.

I.

"I keep working in and out of terrible fits of depression followed by times when I am happy and work very freely," wrote Sherwood Anderson in 1919. "Business and business life [are] more dreadful than ever. There are moments when I even play with the idea of suicide as a way of escape." [3] Such times of desperation came frequently to Sherwood Anderson in his adult life, and their recurrence explains the writer's rebellion against whatever forces seemed to be immediately putting onto his back "the black dog of despair."

The most crucial of Anderson's seasons of despair had occurred on November 27, 1912, when he walked out of the office of his

1. Sherwood Anderson, *Winesburg, Ohio* (New York: B. W. Huebsch, 1919), p. 48.
2. *Ibid.,* pp. 19–20.
3. Letter to Waldo Frank, [May, 1919].

products-distribution company in Elyria, Ohio, and wandered for three days a victim of amnesia. This breakdown, resulting from Anderson's unhappiness with his business and his marriage, became for a generation of American youth the symbolic rejection of the small-town, middle-class life that had once been the goal recommended for, if not always accepted by, "sensible" men and women. Anderson moved in 1913 to Chicago, where he lived by writing advertising copy, the same work he had done there from 1900 to 1904, before his first marriage and his business career in Ohio.

Because the world of business was never congenial to Sherwood Anderson, he managed through writing and through association with the leaders of the Chicago Renaissance to escape into the world of artistic labor that relieved his dissatisfaction with a business career. Anderson had written two novels—*Windy McPherson's Son* [4] and *Marching Men* [5]—while operating his company in Ohio. In Chicago he wrote parts of *Mid-American Chants* [6] and some of the Winesburg stories as early as 1915, but it was the publication of *Winesburg, Ohio* in 1919 that ultimately gave him the social and literary fame that he avidly sought. The act of writing poetry and fiction saved Anderson from the ultimate escape: "Of course there is no such prospect [of suicide], as that would not help and there is so much eager life I want to find my way into. And I am not always depressed. There are days when I ride like a boat on top of it all." [7]

But such days of happiness were rare for Sherwood Anderson. He had begun to think of abandoning Chicago and New York, where he worked briefly in 1918, and of returning to small-town life. "There is the beginning of a scheme on foot by which I may go to live for two or three years in a small Kentucky town," Anderson wrote to Waldo Frank in May, 1918. "If I do you shall come to visit me." As he explained this plan, "The country thing would not take me out of business. I would merely be living in a small quiet place. Would have to do much the same kind of work as I do here. I figure I would not wear myself out so much." [8]

4. New York: John Lane Company, 1916.
5. New York: John Lane Company, 1917.
6. New York: John Lane Company, 1918.
7. Letter to Waldo Frank, [May, 1919].
8. Letter to Waldo Frank, June 5, 1918.

Although this particular plan did not work out for Anderson, he continued to dream of recapturing the life of his boyhood home town. Clyde, Ohio, had been the home of the Anderson family from 1884, when Sherwood was eight years old, until 1895, when his greatly overworked mother died and the family began to disintegrate. As a boy Anderson had often missed school in order to work at a variety of jobs around Clyde, which in the 1880's and the 1890's was undergoing the slow, inevitable transformation from an agricultural to an industrial economy. The town's change from a basically rural to a partly urbanized way of life became the subject of Sherwood Anderson's third novel, *Poor White*, published in 1920.[9] Anderson had begun in the early 1920's to earn a modest profit from his stories of small-town life, he had visited Europe in 1921 as the guest of Paul Rosenfeld, and he had been able by 1923 to abandon the advertising business.

But Sherwood Anderson continued to relive memories of his youth in a rural, late-nineteenth-century America. In 1924 he published *A Story Teller's Story*,[10] a sensitive recreation of his boyhood in Ohio; and in 1926 there appeared *Tar: A Midwest Childhood*.[11] However, Anderson had by 1926 suffered again from very serious disappointments. His second marriage had ended in divorce in 1924, and he had married for a third time. Such friends as William Faulkner and Ernest Hemingway had proved to be ungrateful for Anderson's encouragement and his help with their early publishing. His fourth novel, *Many Marriages*,[12] had been a critical and financial disaster. Most serious of all, the author was overcome with a sense of creative exhaustion, a knowledge that he had for too long been separated from the country people whose lives had been the subjects for his best writing.

The first step toward Anderson's "return to Winesburg" was a vacation spent with his wife in the summer of 1925 near the village of Troutdale, in Grayson County, Southwest Virginia. The Andersons lived in the farmhouse of the John Greear family, located on a hill overlooking Troutdale and the surrounding Blue Ridge Mountains. "It's sweet to see the rains over the hills, hear the sounds at

9. New York: B. W. Huebsch.
10. New York: B. W. Huebsch.
11. New York: Boni and Liveright.
12. New York: B. W. Huebsch.

night," Anderson wrote of mountain life. "It may be that as we get older we draw closer to nature. The cabin where I go to write (it costs me nothing) is a deserted one in a big cornfield on top of a mountain. Cowbells in the distance, the soft whisper of the corn." [13]

As Sherwood Anderson was completing *Tar,* he became fascinated with his Virginia neighbors. "The mountain people are sweet," he wrote. "No books, little false education, real humbleness. It does so beat talking to pretentious half-artists. We may try to acquire a few acres and a cabin. Hills everywhere with cold springs trickling out of them, forests yet. People live in isolated cabins far apart. Everyone wants you to come in, to drink moonshine, to eat, to spend the night." [14]

Before leaving Virginia, Anderson did buy a small farm near Troutdale, where he planned to build what would be his only permanent home. He spent the winter in New Orleans, enjoying the success of *Dark Laughter,*[15] his only best-selling novel; and in the spring of 1926 he returned to his Virginia farm to oversee the building of "Ripshin," named for a mountain stream that bounded his property. A large country house of hand-hewn logs, timbers, and stones, "Ripshin" was carefully built for Sherwood Anderson by self-trained mountain craftsmen, and its construction required most of the ten thousand dollars he had made from *Dark Laughter.*

But, as "Ripshin" neared completion, Sherwood Anderson entered a time of even greater depression. His brother Earl, always jealous of Sherwood's success, became seriously ill. Anderson began to worry over the three children of his first marriage, at a time when his third marriage was becoming unsatisfactory. A trip to Europe in the winter of 1926–27 did not relieve his despair, for he returned to Virginia to face a greater problem, the necessity of fulfilling the terms of a contract with his publisher. According to an agreement with the firm of Boni and Liveright—to last from May 1, 1925, until May 1, 1930, and in return for drawing a weekly advance of one hundred dollars—Anderson was to produce annually one novel or one full-length memoir. Such forced labor soon became weari-

13. Letter to Alfred Stieglitz, August 14, 1925. In *Letters of Sherwood Anderson,* edited by Howard Mumford Jones and Walter B. Rideout (Boston: Little, Brown and Company, 1953), p. 145.
14. *Ibid.*
15. New York: Boni and Liveright, 1925.

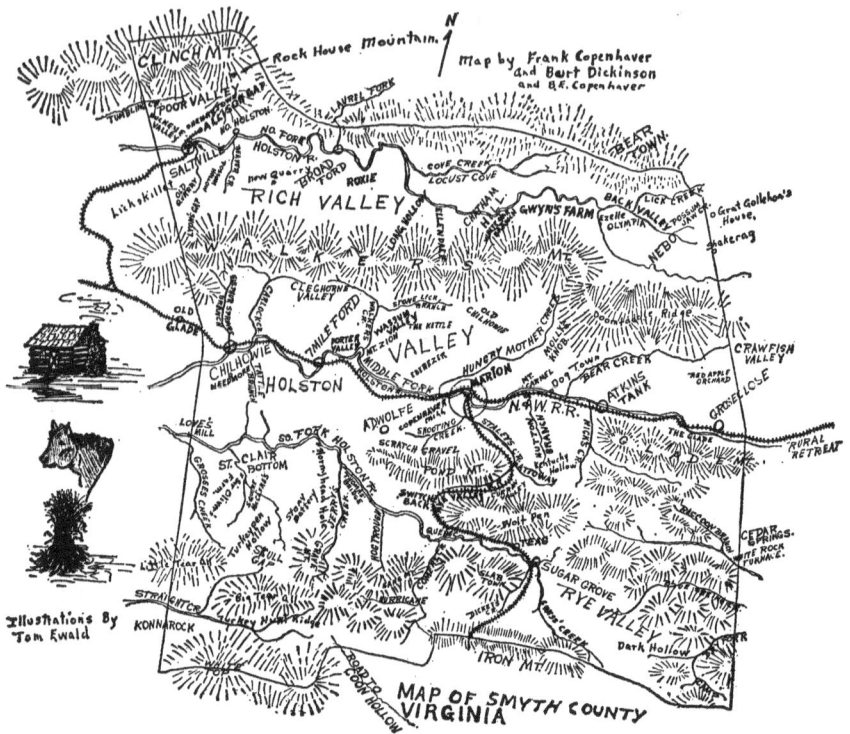

Map of Smyth County, Virginia, Drawn by Marion Natives for Hello
Towns! (1929)

some to Anderson, who wrote in the fall of 1927, "I have decided
that, for my soul's good, I have got to give up the notion of living by
writing. This idea that one must produce constantly or starve is
terribly detrimental to any sort of freedom of approach. . . . I have
decided for my own good I have to begin making my living." [16]

But what work could there be in rural Southwest Virginia for a
famous author who, at the age of fifty-one, could not face a return to
business and who was unskilled at any trade other than writing?
Sherwood Anderson found the answer to this question when he
attended a country fair in Smyth County, Virginia, a few miles from
"Ripshin."

Marion, Virginia, a pleasant town on the Holston River, between

16. Letter to Ralph Church, September 28, 1927.

the Walker and the Clinch ranges of the Blue Ridge Mountains, in
1927 claimed approximately four thousand people, most of whom
lived by operating small businesses to serve the farmers of Smyth
County. The main street of Marion is part of U.S. Highway
Eleven, which, along with the Norfolk and Western Railway,
brings tourists and traffic through the town. When Sherwood Anderson came to Marion, he found in the county seat several colonial
houses, two hotels, a junior college, a furniture factory, and a state
mental hospital.

In 1927 the Smyth County Fair was held in Marion from August 30 through September 3. On one of those days, while sitting in
the grandstand watching a trotting race, Sherwood Anderson met
Denny Culbert of Marion. Anderson talked with Culbert of his
need to find work to support him until he could again depend on
his writing for a living. By chance Culbert knew that the two small
weekly newspapers in Marion were for sale. He suggested that
Anderson consider buying them, and two months later Sherwood
Anderson was a small-town newspaper editor.[17]

Leaving the fairground immediately, Anderson went to the office
of the *Marion Democrat* and the *Smyth County News*. "I was
excited and a little frightened," he later recalled, and his first sight
of the Marion Publishing Company was not inspiring: "The office
of the papers was just off the main street of the town and faced the
county jail and there were churches all about. There was the
county court house, a quite dignified looking stone building, facing
the main street, and back of that the jail with a vacant lot, filled at
that time with the town's road building machinery, between the jail
and the low brick building containing the newspaper plant, and
clustered about these the Lutheran, the Presbyterian and the Bap-
tist churches."[18]

Arthur L. Cox had published the *Smyth County News* and the
Marion Democrat since 1921. Apparently, no one in Smyth
County had thought it odd that a Republican and a Democratic
paper came from the same printshop and contained material almost

17. Robert Lane Anderson, Obituary for Sherwood Anderson, *Smyth County
News*, March 13, 1941, p. 6.
18. "How I Ran a Small Town Newspaper," Newberry Library MS, p. 4.

identical except for political editorials. Although the two newspapers were poorly run and heavily indebted, Cox asked Sherwood Anderson to pay twenty-five hundred dollars for each of them.

On one of his frequent trips to New York, Anderson had become acquainted with Burton Emmett, head of a large advertising company. Emmett had liked the writer and had asked to buy some of his manuscripts and personal letters. Anderson never understood why his manuscripts should appeal to anyone or how they could be intrinsically valuable, but Burton Emmett came to have an absolute passion for any piece of paper written on by Sherwood Anderson. The businessman agreed to lend the author five thousand dollars with which to buy the *Marion Democrat* and the *Smyth County News*. In return Anderson promised to repay the interest-free loan in two installments in either four or five years, to send Emmett original manuscripts of his own published and unpublished work, and to try to persuade other authors to sell their manuscripts and letters to the collector. This agreement was to last "until my obligation to you is cleared up and as long as you and I live." [19]

Sherwood Anderson had his newspapers. He had made arrangements, borrowed money, signed notes and documents, and promised to pay back money which he very well might never have. But he was at last the owner, editor, and publisher of the only newspapers in Marion and Smyth County, Virginia: ". . . presently there I was, sitting on my throne, an editor at last, a man in a great tradition. The figures of old Ben Franklin, Dana, Bennett, Horace Greeley, Colonel Watterson seemed to be walking before me up and down between the makeup stones and the type cases of my dark little shop." [20]

Sherwood Anderson was not a citizen of Marion, and he had certainly never before thought of how issues of newspapers are born. The new editor was, therefore, appropriately awed by the task that he faced: "I was to become a moulder of public opinion, a

19. Letter to Burton Emmett, October 24, 1927. The exact financial arrangements that Sherwood Anderson made in buying the two papers are not completely clear. Anderson wrote in 1931 of having paid fifteen thousand dollars for the printshop and the newspapers and of having assumed three thousand dollars in debts: "Of this I borrowed $4,000 at a bank here, gave the man $7,000 in notes and put in $4,000 of my own." This and the subsequent discussion of Anderson's financial actions are from his letter to Will Alexander, January 3, 1931.
20. "How I Ran a Small Town Newspaper," p. 5.

figure in the social scheme of the community. Having done this thing, made the plunge, I was at once doubtful, and a good deal frightened. What would the people of the town think of me as editor? On that first day . . . I thanked Heaven that I had taken charge on Friday . . . my two papers were both weeklies, one issuing on Tuesday, the other on Thursday . . . I would have time in any event to get my breath." [21]

II.

As the new editor of the *Smyth County News* and the *Marion Democrat,* Sherwood Anderson had an adequate printshop equipped with a five-thousand-dollar linotype, a job-printing press, a flat-bed press and paper folder, sufficient fonts of type, and a crew of journeymen helpers. Knowing that he could never profit from his newspapers, he planned to take from the business only his living expenses. The previous editor had invested as little money as possible in his work, for he had considered the printshop no more than a money-making institution. Even so, the man's business sense had failed him.

When Sherwood Anderson took charge of the *Marion Democrat* and the *Smyth County News,* the yearly subscription price was $1.25. Checking the lists of readers revealed that even this small price was often not collected; some subscriptions had been unpaid for ten years. Anderson's first act as editor was to increase the subscription rate to $1.75 per year, payable in advance. The move was calculated, he explained, to make people "want" to read the newspapers and to convince businessmen that advertising in them was worthwhile. The new policy was successful because the quality of the papers improved immeasurably under Anderson, not because the new editor was Sherwood Anderson, for, he declared, "not three people in the county had heard of me."

Doubtless, the political fairness that Anderson exercised contributed to the success of his newspapers. The previous editor had published an eight-page Republican *News* and a four-page *Democrat,* always pushing subscribers toward the former. To prevent the threatened establishment of a new Democratic paper, Anderson made both papers eight-page issues and insisted that all political

21. *Ibid.*

comment be confined to the political editorials. Sherwood Anderson solved the problem of writing partisan editorials by having the local sheriff write politically for the *Marion Democrat* and the town's postmaster for the *Smyth County News.*

When Anderson bought the *Democrat* and the *News,* the general assumption was that the novelist must somehow have already acquired a thorough knowledge of editing and publishing newspapers, but the closest Sherwood Anderson had ever come to any sort of printing was mailing manuscripts to his own publishers and writing advertising copy in Chicago. As a newspaper editor, he admitted to "feeling our way along" from the time he bought the papers until he stopped working with them. However, Anderson came to have distinctive ideas about country journalism.[22]

According to Sherwood Anderson, the story of country newspapers was one of sudden decline. He admitted that many of the early American weekly newspapers were merely political organs, but among the early country editors Anderson found "many sharp, shrewd men . . . some of the great writers, violent men filling their little sheets with violent tirades, editors controlled by state politicians, others because of their wit and humor becoming national figures."

These idealized, frontier varieties of early American editors had played important roles, Anderson believed: "The small town editor, with his little four, six, or eight page paper was the voice of the big outside world coming in." The country editor was usually a man with political aspirations; often he became a member of Congress: "He got railroad passes, could travel up and down his state, go to political conventions. Being a small town editor pretty much meant also being a politician." The local weekly flourished at a time "when the state and national politicians, going from town to town, on speech making tours, could present a new face to every community, a time when few people in the towns took daily newspapers, when there were few telephones . . . and then a change came as changes do come quickly in American life."

22. "The American Small Town: Meet the Editor," Newberry Library MS, p. 4. The subsequent summary of Anderson's history of country journalism is paraphrased and quoted from this manuscript, pp. 4–7, and from *Home Town* (New York: Alliance Book Corporation, 1940), pp. 104–8. No information is extant on possible sources for Anderson's theories.

The time of this change was "after the 1880's, when the surge of the small towns to the cities was at its height, when the American small town weekly began to go downhill." Young men who would have begun a career of writing by reporting for country papers went instead to neighboring cities to work for large daily newspapers. Selling "patent insides" or "boilerplate"—whole articles or pages mass-produced and ready to print—became a huge business, spreading the dullness attendant on such material. The linotype machine replaced the journeyman printer, and publishing local papers became a business for job-printers, men who cared little for high standards of journalism. The country weeklies were merged into chains by syndicates; and, "much of the old humanism, wit and humor of the old time country editor quite gone, the Heywood Brouns, the Frank Adams, the Cappers, the O. O. McIntyres and Pegglers who in another age might have stayed in the towns, become editors of small town weeklies, became city newspaper columnists, writing for syndicates." These factors all worked together to cause the gradual decline of country journalism until one paper resembled every other paper, until standardization characterized still another area of life in the United States.

Warning about the dangers inherent in the commercialization and the standardization of life in America is perhaps the predominant concern of Sherwood Anderson in all of his writing. As early as 1921, he had become mildly alarmed about the increasing loss of individuality in modern newspapers. In one of the rare comments that Anderson made about newspapers before becoming a country editor himself, the author wrote, "In my own father's day . . . there was not a man of our Ohio town, counting himself at all a person of intelligence, who did not know the name of the editor of every outstanding New York, Chicago, Cincinnati or New Orleans newspaper." [23] These editors were strongly individualistic men who continually tried to appeal from their informed, complex minds to readers across the nation. The modern newspaperman, Anderson found, could not be discovered through the contents of his paper; no one cared who published his news or what the editor thought: "A man doesn't think of personalities in connection with newspa-

23. *Sherwood Anderson's Notebook* (New York: Boni and Liveright, 1926), pp. 139–40.

pers anymore, of the old type of unique individuals impressing
their personalities on people in general through the ownership of
newspapers." [24]

Sherwood Anderson determined that his own country weeklies
should not be typically colorless newspapers. On one of his first
subscription blanks the new editor spoke:

> The Smyth County News is a local town newspaper, published weekly
> at Marion, Virginia, and circulating largely in Smyth County and in
> neighboring counties. It is filled for the most part with local news.
> Births and deaths, what the churches are doing, the price of farm
> products.
> Who gets hurt during the fall threshing or shoots some fellow for
> getting gay with his wife.
> School news, sports, visits.
> The aim of this paper is to give expression to the joys and sorrows,
> the political fights, all of the everyday life of a very typical American
> community.
> The paper is owned and edited in every way except politically—by
> Sherwood Anderson, sometimes favorably, often unfavorably known as
> a novelist and story teller.
> He does not claim to be a poet.
> Also he will try to induce his friends among other American writers
> to send things in to us.
> The subscription price to those at a distance is $2.00 a year.
> Our own home folks we will charge less. [25]

Anderson knew that the country weekly, when compared to the
city daily, was not in the usual sense a newspaper. Even in its
mechanical aspects, the weekly should not attempt to imitate the
daily paper. He thought of the country newspaper as "a kind of big
weekly county letter" [26] which must have in its pages some news for
every reader: "One of the ways in which a country editor insures
having a good circulation is by getting into each issue as many
names as possible." [27] The news reported in each issue must be
intensely local. News of events on the state, national, and interna-
tional levels must be drastically condensed or usually not even
mentioned: "We tell everyone in the county about people's small

24. *Ibid.*, p. 140.
25. "Grass Roots News," Newberry Library Anderson Papers.
26. "The Country Weekly: The Harris Lectures, Number II, Northwestern
University," Newberry Library MS, p. 13.
27. *Ibid.*

doings, when they kill hogs, begin planting corn, go visiting, etc." [28]

Sherwood Anderson did not try to compete with city dailies. He advised his readers that if they wanted state and national news they should subscribe to some metropolitan paper or to a national magazine. Most country editors then used the cheap "ready-made insides" that required no work before printing, but Anderson had a continuing horror of such standardized material as pineapple recipes, bankers' propaganda, and cheap fiction. This "boilerplate" was free to publishers, but Anderson preferred to fill his newspaper columns with more enlightening reading. Among the articles that Anderson printed in his *Smyth County News* were, for example, the Book of Ruth; George Moore's "A Story"; "Death," a poem by Maxwell Bodenheim; Chateaubriand's letter to Monsieur de Marcellus on how to appreciate cats; "Crime and the Public" by Max Radin; and several of his own stories, including "The Untold Lie" from *Winesburg, Ohio*. Whether the local farmers, blacksmiths, and waitresses enjoyed, understood, or even read an Anderson or Turgenev story that completely covered with fine print a whole page of newspaper is doubtful; but the editor enjoyed playing literary mentor to his unsophisticated readers.

Besides printing items of literature in the *Marion Democrat* and the *Smyth County News*, Sherwood Anderson kept in his printshop nearly a thousand books to serve as a public lending library. These books were usually donated to the author by various publishing firms, and the newspapers regularly carried descriptions of new additions to what then served as Marion's only public library. The shop itself become a social center for the town, rivaling the drugstore and the courthouse steps as a popular meeting place. "There is a big stove in the center of the room," Anderson wrote, "and there are books here to be read and pictures on the walls. Nowadays you can get good colored prints of modern painting at little cost. We have Van Goghs, Cézannes, Marins, Gauguins, Renoirs. People come in and stare at these paintings but they are interested. . . . There are political discussions, stories told, news of the county is brought in. I swear you'd be surprised. There is a workman's wife here who reads Dostoyevsky." [29]

28. Letter to Will Alexander, January 3, 1931.
29. "The Country Weekly," MS p. 15.

The people of Southwest Virginia appreciated their new editor, even if they were suspicious of his literary works and his private affairs. They learned that Sherwood Anderson intended to have great fun running his *News* and *Democrat*, and they came to know that his purpose was, as one citizen wrote, to "make fun for us, and not just of us." [30] Anderson's policy of reporting only local news appeared sensible to the citizens of Marion: "All of us sufficiently above the illiterate line take a daily paper. It comes on the early train from Roanoke or Richmond. A few of us even get one on the night train from New York or Washington." [31] Because local news was usually known as soon as it was done, people looked forward to seeing it in print, transformed by Anderson into quite interesting and often almost unfamiliar material.

From his own experience Sherwood Anderson was always ready to extoll the advantages of the life of a country editor. From his point of view as a serious writer, Anderson believed that working for local papers was a marvelous opportunity: "You are in touch with life. You see life, in the towns and on the farms as it is carried on. There is your school for your writers to go to. You are part of it." [32] He often wrote of the difficult life that the artist must lead in America, where "we . . . respect our writers both too much and too little," [33] where the writer is too much worshiped as a sage and too much impoverished as a businessman. However, the young writer could escape social alienation as the editor of the newspaper in his small town: "Gradually as you live and work in a community you come to feel that your town and your county . . . the people living in the little cross roads towns in your county, the men you go fishing with and discuss politics with, the women you meet in the stores and on the streets, the farmers who come into your print shop and whose grim year after year struggle with nature you begin to understand a bit, the children of the town and county, all of these become a part of a family of which more and more you want to feel yourself one too." [34]

Sherwood Anderson seldom played reformer in his newspapers.

30. L. R. Dickinson, "Smyth County Items," *Outlook*, CXLVIII (April 11, 1928), 581.
31. *Ibid.*, p. 583.
32. "The Country Weekly," MS p. 14.
33. "Journalism and the Young Writer," Newberry Library MS, p. 7.
34. *Ibid.*, p. 8.

He avoided political disputes and nailed no slogan to his mastheads. But he valued his newspaper writing, believing that ". . . there may be an opportunity for as good writing in weekly newspapers of this kind as in the magazines or in books." [35] On the many weeks when there might be no real news for his columns the editor was free to "write about what [comes] into his head. We were and are running our own country weeklies as literary adventures too. Why not? We want to make them good reading." [36]

Anderson became so enthusiastic about the opportunities in country journalism that he tried in the early 1930's to interest Julius Rosenwald and Will Alexander in starting funds for the purpose of helping country newspapers. Interested young men were to borrow from the foundations in order to buy or start newspapers in small towns throughout America. Although the Depression of 1929 precluded the possible interest of philanthropists in such schemes, Anderson continued to have great hope for country journalism: "Sometimes I think that the American country press is to-day the biggest, the most pregnant, and the most overlooked opening there is in all American life for young men and women who would like to live and who while they are living would like to get a bit more fun and meaning out of their lives." [37]

Sherwood Anderson wrote to Gertrude Stein of the satisfactions that were his as a reporter for his small-town newspapers:

Been sitting all day in the court room hearing a murder trial, and half sick that nothing I write seems as vital—
These running nerves an alleyway to my little shop.
I surely will send a paper and now. We are just getting one out.
The town band is practicing. It is night. The town is full of people.
I am sent for to sheep shearings, cattle judgings—to see apple tree blossoms. Whatever happens my phone rings. "Come out here and see this, see that." Usually I go.[38]

III.

It is fortunate that until November, 1927, when he faced having to write and print the first issues of the *Marion Democrat* and the *Smyth County News*, Sherwood Anderson really had never

35. *Nearer the Grass Roots* (San Francisco: Westgate Press, 1929), p. 15.
36. "The City Daily: The Harris Lectures, Number I, Northwestern University," Newberry Library MS, p. 16.
37. "The Country Weekly," *Forum*, LXXV (April, 1931), 213.
38. Letter to Gertrude Stein, [1928].

thought much about what a good newspaper should be. He knew
only that for over a decade he had been writing novels and short
stories that the public had enjoyed and that the literary critics had
often praised. It was natural that the author of such fiction should
regard writing for his newspapers as an opportunity to continue
telling good stories well. He saw in the lives of the citizens of
Marion and Smyth County, Virginia, more stories than he would
ever have the time to tell or the bravery to publish. Thus, lacking
any formal training in editing newspapers, the author created two
country weeklies that are distinct products of the mind of Sherwood Anderson.

It would be difficult to call any issue of the *Marion Democrat* or
the *Smyth County News* a typical example of Anderson's newspapers. Each issue was a new challenge to the writer, who had to
gather his own news, write every story in the papers,[39] and see each
issue through the presses. Because Anderson could not afford to
hire a reporter, he traveled about Marion, collecting news from the
courthouse, the drugstore, and street-corner conversations, believing
that "the country newspaper is the drug store; it is the space back of
the stove in the hardware store; it is the farm house kitchen." [40] The
facts which the editor collected were usually more items of gossip
than news, but this stray information was enough framework upon
which Sherwood Anderson could build a story.

The *Marion Democrat* and the *Smyth County News* usually
contained the same material. The printing plates for the Tuesday
Democrat were either left unchanged or merely moved about to
allow room for different mastheads and appropriate political editorials in the Thursday *News*. The four (later eight) pages of the
Democrat and the eight pages of the *News* contained few pictures
because in 1927 small-town newspapers could not afford to illus-
trate many news items. The short articles that Anderson had written on the life of his town and county for the past week were
arranged at random throughout the pages of the newspapers. As

39. Except for some community news items, submitted by cross-roads corre-
spondents; farm news, supplied by the local agricultural office; signed contributions and reprintings; and political editorials, written by the local party men. Most
of the poetry that appeared in Anderson's newspapers was contributed by "Jay G.
Sigmund," really Sherwood Anderson. Samples of it may be found in *Hello
Towns!* (New York: Horace Liveright, 1929).
40. "On Being a Country Editor," Newberry Library MS, p. 5.

one story was usually as important as any other, there were seldom any real headlines.

Typographically, the *News* and the *Democrat* were not attractive. The linotype machine guaranteed even columns of type, six single columns constituting each page. However, the mastheads and running titles often re-used the last week's date, running heads were seen inverted, pages repeated numbers or had irregular numbering, the editor's spellings conformed to those of no known dictionary, and the flat-bed press sometimes inked newsprint in its own whimsical manner. But Sherwood Anderson could not regard the existence of such trifles as serious enough to demand his closer supervision of printing. He preferred to gather and write the news.

An item of news written by Sherwood Anderson combines the characteristics of the short story with those of the familiar essay. As a short story one of Anderson's news articles consists of a few brief sentences that establish scene and mood and lead to the episode that seizes the reader's interest. Then follows a description of the climactic scene, after which the action is explained or the mystery is solved. As a familiar essay the Sherwood Anderson newspaper story makes no pretense at objectivity: the facts are usually included, but they are related by an author who everywhere intrudes to explain the news from his own point of view. Anderson revealed from the first lines of his columns that actual happenings were not his primary concern. The editor's role was to present the events of the town and county as he reacted to them and as he expected his readers to react. Thus most of the stories in the *Marion Democrat* and the *Smyth County News* are graceful, rambling, comic views of life in a small mountain town; or they are wise and tender expressions of sympathy for the sadness that lives in the same town. They usually display as much of Sherwood Anderson as they do of the real news of the week.

Any event, however minor, was of interest to Anderson—a hen that laid an egg on Main Street (Anderson's "Rialto"), the visit to Marion of a mysterious master checker player or a band of gypsies, the courtroom trials that were often pathetic or hilarious, and even the Christmas dinner served to the inmates of the town's jail. The editor ran his country newspapers as though Smyth County, Virginia, were indeed the center of his universe. He attended meetings of the local Kiwanis Club, reported gossip from the drugstore and the courthouse, and drove about the county with the sheriff and the state farm agent. Sherwood Anderson thus made his newspapers good reading, but he was never able to make of them a public forum. The *News* and the *Democrat* became and remained instead a forum for Sherwood Anderson, one in which he wrote what amounted to a weekly diary, a voice for notes out of his life and thought. In his regular "What Say!" editorials and anywhere else in the papers, the editor expressed his love for Southwest Virginia, the troubles and delights of the printshop and his own place in the town, and gently didactic lessons for the culturally deprived mountaineers. "The idea," Anderson wrote, "is to try to catch the color, the smell, the feel of the everyday life of everyday people." [41]

But what of the life of the imagination?

"Having lifted the reader out of the reality of daily life," Sherwood Anderson had stated in 1924, "it is entirely possible for the writer to do his job so well that the imaginative life becomes to the reader for the time real. Little real touches are added. The people of the town—that never existed except in the fancy—eat food, live in houses, suffer, have moments of happiness and die. To the writer, as he works, they are very real. The imaginative world in which he is for the time living has become for him more alive than the world of reality can ever become." [42] And when Anderson wrote for his newspapers he created an imaginary world that existed alongside the area's real life.

"As I couldn't afford a reporter I invented one . . . a purely mythical being," [43] Sherwood Anderson wrote of "Buck Fever," who appeared in the third issue of the *Smyth County News* and the *Marion Democrat*, inspired, the editor later declared, "perhaps . . . from the comic strip in our dailies." [44] Buck Fever was a young mountain man from Coon Hollow, Virginia, where Paw Fever was proprietor of the general store, called after Fever and Ague. Buck had a mother, Malaria Fever; a sister, Spring Fever; and an aunt, Miss Bone Fever—all proudly of the Fever Family of Virginia. He had left behind him in Coon Hollow such family friends as Miss

41. *Home Town*, p. 104.
42. *Sherwood Anderson's Notebook*, pp. 74–75.
43. Letter to Ralph Church, December 22, 1927.
44. Letter to Jacques Chambrun, [May (?), 1939]. In *Letters*, p. 440.

Holly Tawney, Miss Hyacinth Wormwood, Old Miss Sue Thomson, and Uncle Henry Wormwood; and he had come to Marion to work for Sherwood Anderson's newspapers—at outrageously low wages, the subject of complaint frequently published by Buck.

Buck, as his creator made him, "was a young man of eighteen. He was, like most mountain men, a tall lean one and, like most mountain men also, he was shrewd. He had a girl up there, in the mountain hollow, to whom he wished to be true but he was ambitious and to him coming to live in our town and to work for me, being from the first day my star reporter, was a kind of going into the big time." [45] Buck's first newspaper items were merely sportive columns that he wrote as stand-in for Sherwood Anderson. Later he underwent a brief period of writing in dialect, but soon Buck was a citizen of Marion, one who knew the people his boss knew and who could write comically about any happening. "Buck could say things about people, make cracks at them, have fun at people's expense that, had I been writing under my own name, would have at once got me into trouble," [46] Anderson explained, and he went on to create other imaginary characters.

There soon appeared in the pages of the *Marion Democrat* and the *Smyth County News* Mrs. Homing-Pigeon, a cultivated, refined southern lady who took great interest in public affairs. Colonel Star Dust worked in a local bank but was most interested in astronomy. The mysterious Black Cat of Chilhowie had thirteen kittens and traveled U.S. Highway Eleven at a speed of thirteen miles an hour. And the Deep Sea Club met regularly in landlocked Smyth County.

Recalling these characters, Anderson said, "There was this imagined life going on in our town and based on the real life of the town. It was rather fun. I think we all enjoyed it and I think also that it was pretty healthy. And we got some things done. It wasn't all play." [47] One project undertaken by Buck Fever, Mrs. Homing-Pigeon, and the editor was making of the machinery dump opposite Marion Publishing Company a presentable town park: "We began to write of it. We kept it up week after week. We just assumed that

45. "How I Ran a Small Town Newspaper," p. 9.
46. *Ibid.*
47. *Ibid.*, p. 11.

the park was already there. We spoke of sitting on the benches in the park on hot summer evenings, of tired farm women who had come into town resting there, of children playing in the park. We spoke of flower bordered paths, of roses blooming and of the flowering bushes and presently it worked. We got our park. We had fixed the charming little park in the imagined life of the people of the town and, after a time, the fact that it had not been built became unbearable to them." [48] Anderson named the new common "Henry Mencken Park," but the townspeople gratefully renamed it "Sherwood Forest."

IV.

"As I told you before," Sherwood Anderson explained to one of his sons, "I have come here and taken hold of these papers because, having nothing to do but write, I found myself unable to do that. In the end perhaps a man has to manufacture his own interest in life. A young man thinks he wants fame. I have had that. It amounts to nothing. What does? God knows what except work." [49]

The year 1928 was one of Anderson's happiest times, for publishing the *Marion Democrat* and the *Smyth County News* gave him the opportunities he had longed for: he had been able to earn his living at some trade other than writing for New York publishers, and he had managed to regain a close relationship with the people of an American small town. The newspaper editor had made himself an accepted and welcome member of his mountain community.

Thus Sherwood Anderson responded with angry amazement to an offer to sell his two country newspapers:

I have got an occupation here, something to do, I like the smell of the shop, the business, the uncertainty, the position it has given me in the community. . . .

I must have a job and I never have had another job that gave me half so much pleasure.

A man has to work. He cannot be just a teller of tales. He has to find somewhere a place into which he fits. [50]

Much of Sherwood Anderson's early writing had been a condemnation of many aspects of life in the small towns of America. He

48. *Ibid.*
49. Letter to John Anderson, [1928].
50. "I Will Not Sell My Papers," *Outlook*, CL (December 5, 1928), 1287.

had become disillusioned with the materialism, the hypocritical puritanism, and the exaggerated self-importance of the villager. However, the author's decision to live in Southwest Virginia had resulted from his later realization that all of the positive qualities that he admired—individual strength, pride, and tenderness—were to be found in small-town men and women. But Sherwood Anderson's reconciliation with small-town life carried within it the seeds of his second move away from that life. Marion, Virginia, was far removed from the labor agitation, the Great Depression, the socialist movement—all of which Anderson wanted to to understand and needed to be near. Leaving his son, Robert Lane Anderson, to publish the *News* and the *Democrat*, Sherwood began in 1929 to travel widely, writing articles for his newspapers and lecturing often to support himself. Southwest Virginia was to be Sherwood Anderson's home for the rest of his life, but "Ripshin" and Marion were more bases for traveling from than permanent residences.

"Perhaps only a passionate traveler like myself can realize how lucky he is to be able to call a small town his home," Sherwood Anderson wrote shortly before his death in 1941. "My work is constantly calling me away from Marion, but I always hunger to get back. There is in the life of the small town a possibility of intimacy, a chance to know others—an intimacy oftentimes frightening, but which can be healing. . . . A man goes away and comes back. Certain people have died. Babies have been born. Children of yesterday have suddenly become young men and women. Life has been going on. Still nothing has really changed. On the streets, day after day, mostly the same faces. There is this narrow but fascinating panorama. In a way it is too intimate. Life can never be intimate enough." [51] In demonstrating the essential truth of this paradox lies the value of Sherwood Anderson's adventure as a country editor. Never have such people as the residents of Marion and Smyth County, Virginia, forty years ago enjoyed such a rich literature in their weekly newspapers.

51. *The Sherwood Anderson Reader,* edited by Paul Rosenfeld (New York: Houghton Mifflin Company, 1947), pp. 740–41.

1927

OUR NEW EDITOR'S BOW

November 3

I have just acquired the *Smyth County News* and in the future expect to be the managing editor. For two years now I have lived in this section of Virginia.* I came here three years ago on a visit and became enthusiastic about the country and the people. By profession I am a writer. From time to time, for the last ten or fifteen years, I have written and published some dozen or more books. There have been books of essays, poetry, novels, and short stories. My books, published first in America, have also been published in England and translated and published in France, Germany, Spain, Sweden, Russia, Japan, and other European countries.

Since I have been a writer, and during the years before I became a writer, I have lived in various parts of America. Born a small-town man, in an Ohio town about the size of Marion, I afterwards lived

* See below "A Note on Editing," pp. 213–15.

in Europe and in America, in Chicago, New York, San Francisco and New Orleans.

I came into this country in the first place because I had grown tired of city life and wanted the quiet intimacy of life in a smaller place, but having been a busy man all my life I found that my life in the country did not keep me busy enough to be happy.

I had come into this country in the first place on the recommendation of a friend, Mr. Julian Harris, the son of old Joel Chandler Harris, the author of the famous Uncle Remus books.

My father before me was a Southern man * and I have always liked the tone of Southern life.

In acquiring this paper and becoming its publisher, I feel that something should be said to its readers. Although I have lived in this section for two years now, I still feel myself a comparative stranger. In undertaking the publication of this paper I want to keep it an intensely local paper. I want to get into it all the possible news of our own section and of what I have come to think of as my own people. In this I shall need help. I would like to have readers of this paper feel it as his or her paper. If you have suggestions that you think will make the paper more readable and valuable send them in. Send in any item of news that you think will be of interest to other people.

I am taking hold of this paper in the midst of a hot local political fight. I think any of you would resent, and rightfully, my getting personally into this fight. What I shall do about politics is to open the pages of this paper generously to the representative men of the party for which it stands.

In my own editorial columns, written by myself, I shall express myself in my own way on the life about me and on the life of the outside world. Every man has to express his reactions to life as it comes to him through his own eyes. No two of us see things alike. I am taking hold of the papers at a time when they have the largest circulation they have ever had. There is scarcely a home in Marion or in all of the country about Marion which might be thought of as the Marion territory that does not now receive every week its

* Anderson enjoyed cultivating this personal legend about his father, Irwin Anderson, who was born and lived his early life near West Union, Ohio. Only while serving in the Ohio forces during the Civil War did Irwin Anderson travel in the South, primarily in Tennessee and Georgia.

Marion or Smyth County paper. It is for me, I realize, a rare opportunity. I want to draw you all closer to the paper and draw it closer to you.

The community in which this paper is published is a peculiar one in that it is filled with what might nowadays be called Old Americans. People living in this country do not perhaps realize how rapidly that condition has changed in almost every other part of the country. We here in this community should see in that condition something of a challenge, too. If we are Old Americans here in this Virginia Southwest, what is our life like? What are we making of it?

I would like to open the columns of this paper to the expression of all sorts of opinions. The last thing I want is to superimpose my own opinions or my own points of view on my readers. To a certain extent I dare say that can't be helped. I shall try to be as modest and retiring as my own nature will let me be.

Among other things I would like to get the readers of this paper into the habit of writing to the paper and expressing their own opinions. Really, I would like the paper to become a sort of forum, to have every reader feel it as distinctly his paper. If you have something on your chest, get it off. It will be good for you and good for the paper.

However, in taking over the general editorship of the columns of a paper like this, I cannot quite keep myself altogether out of it. No writer is exactly modest, a shrinking flower. If he were he would not become a writer.

But at any rate I ask you all to like me as much as you conveniently can and to help me all you can. In helping me you will be helping your own home paper and a home paper like this should be the voice not of one section of the community but of all sections.

A GREAT MEETING

November 3

Your faithful correspondent was invited to the meeting of the Kiwanis Club at the Methodist church. I have been invited to two of these dinners. They were both so good that I have already planned to join both churches. I may end by joining every church in town if they all set forth such dinners. O, boy.

As to the meeting. Emptying into my wife's lap what small change I had in my pocket, I went. It was a gorgeous meeting. Having been searched, I got in. Doctor Slater was singing. He has a beautiful voice. The club claimed to have some business to do, but I didn't see them do any. Everyone was too festive. I was never in such a place. Every man in Marion must be eloquent. They all wanted to make speeches.

Finally Dr. Slater struggled to his feet; two men tried to hold him down. They couldn't, he was so strong. When he had got through talking there wasn't a dry eye in the house. Great tears were rolling down Mr. Charles Lincoln's bronze cheeks.

To cheer us up, Mr. Frank Lemon, the well-known juggler, got up, taking from his pocket several colored balls, two bowie knives, a pistol, and a half-pint bottle of mountain spring water. He kept them all up in the air for five minutes. It was wonderful; he never cut or wet himself once.

After that, Colonel Tate got up and made a speech. It was about nature. His subject was the hardness of hickory nuts but he broadened it out. For the sake of the sporting men present he explained the difference between a corn shock and a flock of quail. What he said was that you could, if you were careful, go right up to the shock of corn, push it over, and lie down on it, but that you could rarely do this with a flock of quail. It sounded true.

After this, Doctor Slater and George Cook again sang. It was certainly good to see these two boys skipping hand-in-hand barefooted across the floor and up to the platform. It reminded your correspondent of his own innocent youth. They sang several songs, among them one entitled "The Nightingale with Eyes of Blue." Doctor Slater took the part of the nightingale and Mr. George Cook the part of the blue eyes. It was good.

Another and more truthful account of the meeting may possibly be found somewhere else in this paper. The paper is getting so good we can't keep track of it.

FOOLED AGAIN

November 3

Your new editor came into town Monday. Children prancing in the streets at night, dancing, song, laughter, cheers. Girls and boys in fancy costumes.

Fool that I am. I thought it was because all Marion was so glad the new editor had arrived.

It was only Halloween.

MORE NEWS

November 3

Driving along a country road thinking. I have become managing editor of two papers—the *Smyth County News* and the *Marion Democrat*. Each week I want, if possible, to put something personal into these papers. I do not want to make it an expression of opinion. There are thousands of men and women in this and the surrounding counties who have been here longer than I have. I shall try to go very easy in the matter of thrusting myself forward.

However, I was born and have lived all my life in America. Marion is a distinctly American community. We are Old Americans here. The new people who have come into some sections of America so rapidly have not come in here.

In Marion and in the surrounding country you will find every form of present-day American life except perhaps the tremendous problem of the assimilation and understanding of Europeans who have just come to America. Here we have the farm and the factory. New life is flowing in here. Marion is bound to grow. It lies in a great, rich section of what may well be called "underdeveloped America."

And what a lovely country. It was the physical loveliness of this and the surrounding counties that brought me in here. Having come, I did not want to leave. I sought work I could do here, and, seeking such work, bought these papers.

It is my hope to make them the voice of the best impulses of the country, of Southwestern Virginia. To do that I shall have to have help.

First of all, I shall want the news, all of the news. I should like to make all of the readers of these papers feel that they belong to all. I shall want your help. Whatever happens to you, of interest to your neighbors, phone or write to us about it. Help make and keep the papers alive and vital.

Driving along a country road through a lovely community, thinking of what I want to do as editor of these papers. Until I am thoroughly in the saddle I shall print in these pages things that interest me.

An occasional poem that seems to me alive and vital.

I shall occasionally pick up and reprint an old tale.

I want to put into it things seen and felt, strange happenings in this and other communities that have attracted my attention.

As I go along I think I shall reprint here some of my own tales. All my life I have been a story teller, listening to stories, telling stories. I shall hardly be able to keep out of the pages of these papers some of the stories I am constantly picking up.

FINE HUNTING WEATHER

November 17

The opening of the hunting season on Tuesday the 15th saw Marion with a lot of its best citizens missing. Lovers of the dog, the gun, the woods, and the whir of the pheasant or the quail cutting out for cover were up and out early. The sportsmen had fine weather and there were some full game bags before night.

Reports from all over the county and from surrounding counties say that the birds are plentiful this year and that the sportsmen will have a happy season.

Your correspondent is a good hunter but a bum shot. We enjoy hunting the elusive bird. We like to see him fly. We enjoy shooting at him and scaring him. There is one bunch of pheasants over on our hollow we have hunted season after season. We know almost every bird in the flock by his first name. When we do not get out, as we didn't on the opening day this year, it is a bitter disappointment to these birds. They feel they have not been treated as they should be. BUCK FEVER.

AUTUMN

November 24

I do not agree with the poet who termed this season the "melancholy days" and the "saddest of the year."

To me there is no more lovely season, no time when my own thoughts seem more in tune with nature. The frost on the pumpkin; the corn in the shock; the looking forward to happy, lazy hours before the roaring fire, while the wind whistles through the naked trees; the vivid colors of the leaves; and Thanksgiving, and Christmas; and turkey, mince pie, cider and nuts.

And the rosy-cheeked children trooping home from school; football; Halloween, with its witches and goblins; roast apples; and Santa Claus coming.

Old Mother Goose will soon be picking the fluffy down from her geese, to fall in flakes of snow of purest white. Is there anything purer, more lovely, than virgin snow? Who does not love to watch it fall, slowly, silently, until it blankets the dead earth with a mantle of velvety softness?

And the sliding—boys belly-busting; sweethearts holding tightly; the merry screams; the upset in the snow. And the skating on the pond, with the blazing fire to warm by; and then the trudging home in the fading sky.

Nature is taking its rest so that next year it can blossom forth in green glory. The trees and grass and shrubs are asleep—conserving life to emerge again in masses of color.

And the anticipation of spring with its robins and kites and marbles.

No, autumn is not melancholy. The lovely Indian Summer is to me the most charming season of all the year. And I would not live always where there was only one season, no matter how lovely that climate might be. It is the change of time and season that fascinates me, that seems to bring me nearer to nature and its Great Architect.

TRY THIS ON YOUR PIANO

December 1

Dig, ye sheriff, dig;
Dig, ye neighbors, dig.
Digging all day, no sugar in their tea,
When you're working for Smyth County.

Our beloved sheriff doesn't intend always to be a sheriff, picking up bootleggers and all that. There are easier ways of making a living. Look at Gene Tunney and Jack Dempsey.

By the way, sing the above song to the tune of "I Love My Pick But O, You Shovel."

All a man needs to get in the Tunney-Dempsey class is a lot of good exercise. Sheriff Dillard is getting his.

Take last Sunday as an example.

But we had better begin at the beginning and tell you the story.

There are three brothers named Jackson living on Clinch Mountain under the shadow of Red Rock, near Saltville.

About three months ago one of the Jacksons disappeared. No one knows where he went. Probably he just walked off. He may have got a little tired of our country. Before now, your faithful correspondent has done little things like that himself.

But that is neither here nor there. The point is that one of the Jacksons disappeared, vamoosed, lit out, skadoodled.

All quiet on Clinch Mountain. Then a rumor started. It grew and grew. The rumor ran down the mountain into the valleys. The rumor said that the aforesaid Jackson was not vamoosed but dead.

He was dead and buried secretly under the barn at the Jackson place.

You know how rumors grow. This one grew fine. People got excited. Last Sunday morning they disturbed the sleep of Sheriff

Dillard. "Come over here," a tense voice called to him over the long-distance telephone from Saltville.

Always alert to his duty, Sheriff Dillard went. He drove to Saltville and was told the mysterious and horrid tale. Taking under his wing a goodly company of Saltville citizens, including the following, he lit out for Clinch Mountain.

List of illustrious diggers:

Well, there was C. H. Holmes, B. G. Thompson, Sam Dillard, Si Feis, Mr. Cardwell, and several others.

And away they all went. The Jackson place was reached. Picks and shovels were provided. Besides the good diggers from Saltville, others came afoot, on horseback, and in cars. A great concourse gathered. We are told there were so many present that they lifted up the barn and set it over a fence into a nearby field.

Then they began to dig. They dug for hours in the hot sun. They made a great and magnificent hole.

But, alas, no corpse.

They didn't even uncover a mine or a hidden pot of treasure. Nothing came out of the hole but just dirt and a few rocks.

Sheriff Dillard says it is all right with him. He says he needed a little exercise anyway.

"Dig, ye soldiers, dig."

THE FEVER FAMILY

December 1

We are in receipt of a letter signed "Malaria Fever," who says she is the mother of our ready correspondent, Buck Fever.

The letter says:

"I wish you would not let my boy Buck write so much for your papers. I am afraid he may become a newspaper writer. It is a low occupation. We Fevers are of an old Virginia family. I think it is vulgar to be always having our name in the paper."

The Fevers are well known up Coon Hollow way. Buck Fever's father (and, incidentally, the husband of Malaria Fever) is a member of the firm of Fever and Ague. They keep a general store at the head of Coon Hollow.

HUMAN MISERY

December 15

When it sinks low enough and gets caught in the trap of life, human life can be both dangerous and terrible.

Thomas Patterson, who says he is from Martinsville, West Virginia, drifted into town on Monday. The man is a dope. You know what that means. When he got to Marion he was desperate. He went first to the office of Mayor Dickinson and then to Dr. Weindell. The M.D. could not supply him with the drug he craved. He got desperate and ugly and attacked Dr. Weindell, striking him in the face and cutting his lip. Then he fled. It was a brutal and uncalled-for attack.

It would not do, of course, to let such a man run loose. Men and boys took up the chase. Highway policeman Jack Williams, Rush Hayes, Sheriff Dillard—all got busy.

Patterson was cornered at the East End Filling Station and showed fight. He was, however, surrounded, and without further injury to anyone was lodged in jail. Everyone breathed a bit easier.

It happens that yours truly never sees a thing of this sort without an inward shudder. It was a gray, dismal day. I cannot escape this trick of identifying myself with such a poor human. As he runs through the street I imagine myself running. I imagine myself also the victim of some terrible habit, driven to desperation, brutalized. Normal human beings should thank God they are not as this man has become. There are still plenty of problems to be solved.

CATTLE RUSTLER
PICKED UP NEAR MARION

December 22

You don't have to go to the movies to get wild-west life in our little old town. Writers of wild-west tales, come on down here to live. Bring your money with you. We're a little short ourselves. We got excitement here now.

One day last week, Jack Williams, the Lee Highway cop, got word that there was a famous cattle rustler somewhere in this country. Jack got busy, went out and got him, took his guns off him, and brought him in. He picked him up over near Wytheville, but what sort of a place is that to keep a desperate man in? He brought him right on over here to Marion to our own favorite little old county jail. Buck Fever helped him.

Buck says the cattle rustler's name is Sam Russell and that he hales originally from over in Grayson County. He was out West though when he got into this mess. Buck's story is that he rustled a bunch of cattle out in western Missouri, drove them to a strange town, insured them there, getting the insurance money, then drove them to another town and sold them. Buck wanted us to try and do the same thing with this paper and we did approach Mr. Gills, the well-known insurance agent, but he frowned on it.

A Missouri sheriff came to town one day last week and took Sam Russell away. Better not rustle any cattle. You may have to go to Missouri.

I will say that Jailor Hopkins gave us most of the lowdown on this story. Buck Fever got so excited, having a real wild westerner in town, he was a little incoherent.

HANNAH

December 22

Dear Mr. Anderson:

You shouldn't went and put that letter in the paper. I am afraid that you may spoil your paper with too much of that sort of doing and knowing how hard up you be I don't want you to take no chances. I was just thinking the other day that if you'd only come up here about six years sooner you might have bought out the *Troutdale News* before it died out. There'd been a pretty good living in it for a mountain man and you could 'a been nearer where I was.

Since I been thinking things all over I ain't so sure about Buck Fever. I don't believe he's the same Fever I thought he was, but don't make no difference if he does his work all right. 'Course now if he takes to running off queer-like and not telling nobody where he's going or when nor why he may fall down on his job and leave you in a close place. Now I ain't never wrote much for the papers but I know you got to stick right to your job if you get very far with it and I hope Buck don't go and get so struck on some girl that he neglects his job.

I aimed to write you all the news this morning, but I'll swon, I'll certainly swon, it's too cold to try. You tell that Buck he never better get gay with me.

Yours for a happy new year's come-back.

HANNAH STOOTS

THE DAY

December 22

Five or six o'clock in the morning. The sun not yet up. Everything inside is at loose ends. Presently you will gather yourself together for the day. Every day is a something special. It is like a house. The foundations for the day have to be laid; the walls have to be put up.

Men are fortunate who have definite tasks. I have always envied bricklayers. There the bricks are. They are all of one size. You must lay every brick just so. A definite task like that takes your mind off yourself and others. You get up in the morning and begin to lay bricks. As you work, your mind clears. You speak to your fellow workmen. The day gets going all right.

Such people as lawyers, doctors, schoolteachers, bankers, manufacturers, preachers, editors, writers—people whose work is partly at least mental—the tone such people set for their day is all-important.

The task the schoolteacher has to face daily would frighten me. There is a whole room full of people—children. Children are usually quick and responsive. The day starts. What is the teacher's mood? It will affect every one of the pupils.

Formerly, I knew personally a good many actors. I used to go around to see them after the show, in their dressing rooms. There was the actor reading the same parts every evening. No two performances were just alike. There were the same words, the same gestures. Something that should have existed between the actor and his audience would not come to life. Many a time have I seen an actor come off the stage bitterly discouraged. He dropped into a chair. "What a rotten performance I gave tonight," he said, shaking his head.

He was the same man he had been on other nights, was well and strong. What was the matter with him?

It must be that with preachers the same thing happens. The challenge given them is something terrific. We go to hear them, expecting them to give us something we have not got in ourselves—that is to say, the strength and inclination toward gentleness, love, all of the finer attributes.

And they, poor men, have daily to go through the same little annoyances the rest of us do.

The businessman, the head of some large enterprise. What a pack of worries for him! He has not only to think of production but of finance, of holding his men in line, of selling what he manufactures. Some manufacturers get rich. I do not envy them what they have to go through to get there.

The day exists as a day. The sun comes up or it rains or snows. I get up early on some days and walk about in the streets. People look outwardly alike, but inside themselves what is going on? There is in me a great curiosity about people. On the whole, I think it is sympathetic. Often in the early morning I lose courage. I run and grab a book and begin to read or I hurry to my typewriter and begin putting down words as I am doing now.

Any little definite thing I can do helps me in laying the foundation for my own day.

SCANDAL IN TROUTDALE

December 22

There is trouble brewing. A lot of people wonder why we came over here from our quiet valley home in the mountains and plunged into the moil of journalism. The secret threatens to come out. Last week, when we weren't looking, Buck Fever slipped into our quiet family journals a letter addressed to us by Hannah Stoots from Troutdale.

It seems Hannah got a little sentimental. She wanted us to come back over there. She pretended she wanted us to come and hunt rabbits.

Well, we feel that Buck has done us a dirty trick. We suspect he is crazy about Hannah himself. If he thinks he can get on the right side of her by giving us away like that, he is mistaken—or we don't know Hannah.

As to our own feeling about Hannah and her feeling for us, we assure everyone it is absolutely pure. Hannah is herself pure. Our feeling for each other, although deep and strong, is entirely Platonic. It is true that, when we lived in Grayson, the sight of Hannah coming along the road, driving her beautiful team of dapple-gray oxen, often gladdened our heart. We were often lonely there in the mountains and now and then, we admit, we stopped and had conversation with Hannah.

We used to talk mostly about the stars and such things. You know how a man and woman talk to each other when they have one of these philanthropic friendships. Well, that's the way we talked. Buck Fever has not done himself, us, Hannah, or any one else any good by breathing the breath of scandal over our pure relationship. I swear, we feel this morning like firing Buck Fever.

ALAS, POOR NELLIE

December 29

Nellie the printshop cat is gone. She was but a young thing. Some two or three weeks ago Gil Stephenson picked her up one day in the street. She had been dropped or had jumped out of an automobile, a tiny gray thing with soft, friendly eyes.

Gil picked her up and carried her to the shop and we all at once fell in love with her. Every man in the shop was ready at any time to go out and buy her food. She fared well while she was with us, perhaps too well.

One day she had a fit. It was just as the paper was being run off the press, a mad little thing whirling about the floor under our feet.

The fit passed. One of the boys picked her up and laid her on a pile of print. She never had another fit. A consultation was held. She had been given too much food.

A diet was decided upon and Nellie prospered. Her affection seemed inexhaustible. All day she sat on the bookkeeper's desk, on Joe's lap at the linotype, on Gil's makeup table, or on Jack's type-case. Now and then she arose and poked her gray head up under someone's hand. "Well, quit working a moment and pay a little attention to me," she seemed to be saying. Nellie was very feminine surely. She seemed to live for affection. In the morning when I came to the shop she was always on Zeb the print shop devil's lap. "Why don't you sweep up, Zeb?" I said. "The boss will be here pretty soon and he likes things clean. He'll be sore at you." "I can't," Zeb said. "Can't you see Nellie is here in my lap?"

And now Nellie is gone. What happened no one knows. Perhaps the absent-minded boss left the door open. Nellie walked out to get a bit of mountain air. It may be that Pat Collins' dog got after her. Later, after she had quite gone and we all began to be a bit anxious, all sorts of rumors came floating in.

Such and such a gray cat had been seen in such and such a place. It might have been any gray cat. How did we know it was our Nellie? We all went home that night saddened and chastened. There was little sleep. All the printshop crowd waking up in the night to think of Nellie.

Perhaps pursued by dogs, cold and hungry. Hands reached out of beds into the cold darkness, looking for that soft, living little ball of fur and affection.

And the next day, Christmas day, too. Members of the staff wandering one by one down to the cold, silent shop. They all did the same thing. They unlocked the door, went in and called.

Nellie. Nellie. Nellie.

How useless it was. All knew she was not there. She would come back all right but, no doubt, is lost. She may be dead.

On the other hand she may be huddled up in some corner somewhere, cold, frightened, starving.

Well, someone may have picked her up. She may have found

another warm, comfortable home, other hands to stroke her soft young body.

That hope clung to. No one here wants any other cat. We want our Nellie back. BUCK FEVER.

A VISITOR

December 29

The Christmas passed quietly in Marion. It was one of those rare mountain winter days when all the world rejoices. Big attendance in the churches. Children going through the streets with contented-looking faces. Old Santa Claus must have been busy. Christmas trees blossomed in many houses.

The week had started with cold, windy weather, but by the end of the week fine days had come. On Saturday the town was packed with people. The merchants all report a fine Christmas business.

On Christmas Eve and early on Christmas morning young men, dressed in their best, wearing new Christmas ties and mufflers, were hurrying along Main Street with mysterious-looking packages under their arms.

In houses the opening of packages. Suspense, then cries of delight.

Always a few lonely, isolated figures.

Old people whose children have all gone away. Young men and women, far from home.

A stranger came into town driving a fast-looking car. He parked it on Main Street and went for a walk.

Your correspondent saw him walk up the street past the high school and turn up the hill toward the cemetery.

He did not stop at any of the graves but went to the brow of the hill where the road turns and stood for a long time, looking down over the town.

What was in his mind? Who was he? Your correspondent became curious and watched him closely. It was as though he wanted to take in the whole town, live over some past experience here.

Such a cold-acting figure on such a day. The man was well-clad and looked young and strong. After standing and looking at the town for some time, he went rapidly back down into Main Street, into his car, and drove away.

The young man may once have lived here. Queer ideas crossing your correspondent's mind.

That the young man may have done something after he left here and did not want to be known. He had so distinctly the air of having come a long way for that one sweeping look at the town.

It may have been that he once loved a woman here. The woman may have died. We could fancy his remembering walks they had taken together on summer evenings. They may have gone to the same spot he visited yesterday. It may have been there he declared his love for her.

A thousand strange possibilities to such a mysterious visit. It gave a fillip to the day. For some reason, after the strange young man was gone, we were made more glad by the sight of the jolly-looking family groups out walking in the streets or going on visits in their cars.

WHAT THE BOYS IN JAIL HAD FOR CHRISTMAS DINNER

December 29

Not so bad. Started with oysters. Hot slices of the finest Smyth County ham, fried chicken with gravy, mashed potatoes, three or four kinds of hot vegetables, a delicious salad, dumplin's.

Jailor Hopkins, watch us closely next year as Christmas time comes on. If you see us committing some small crime, pick us up. We'll try to get someone to bail us out after Christmas. Remember the name, please. BUCK FEVER.

EXPLAINING BUCK

December 29

In justice to our bright young correspondent, Buck Fever, recently of Coon Hollow, Virginia, we offer an explanation. When Buck first came down here from the Hollow and asked us for a job we were a bit doubtful. Buck is a strong and rather handsome young fellow. Since he has been in town and is a little better dressed, he has been getting notes from some of the town girls.

But, girls, Buck is all business. He is raking the field for news like a fine-tooth comb. Every night he stays up to study. It is hard to see Buck these days without a spelling book and a grammar in his hand. Many times late at night he wakes us up for his little spelling lesson. We predict that, in spite of the jealousy of some of the other people up Coon Hollow way, who can't bear to see a young man rise without knocking, Buck is going to get there.

Besides that, he is strong. If there are any readers of this paper who ever get mad at anything the rest of us say and want to make trouble, I warn them now they will have to deal with Buck.

As for Malaria Fever's objections to the publicity he is getting —well, Malaria Fever, catch up with the modern world. Publicity is food, clothing, shelter, and bedding to a rising newspaperman like Buck.

WORK

December 29

It may be there is nothing else in the world will save a man if he is to be saved but work. Young men writing me letters—"But where am I to find work that will keep me absorbed?"

"Buck Fever" As Drawn by Wharton Esherick

What we all want is a motivating thing. Money isn't enough. Power is a disease. What sensible man really wants power?

Something fine sought for in yourself. The struggle is right there. What work does is to carry you over the dull, terrible times.

Sometimes I think it doesn't matter too much what the work is. A man puts down his head and gets through some way. I keep wondering if other men are always having the enervating sense of guilt that often sweeps over me like a fog.

Guilt that I have been able to do so little with what equipment I have.

Some kind of work, kept at pretty constantly, is the only thing I know of to save me from myself.

1928

NELLIE HOME: The Adventures of Nellie, the Printshop Cat

January 3, Marion Democrat

I am back home. I tell you it pays to advertise. To tell the truth, I never thought my getting away from the printshop the way I did and getting lost would stir up the town of Marion the way it did.

Well, I've got to say the people of Marion are mighty nice people. I've had a big adventure all right but I'm none the worse for it.

So now I think I'll put the story in the paper and tell just how it happened. So here goes.

First of all, it was the boss' fault. He came to the printshop Saturday afternoon before Christmas, when everyone was gone, and started writing some more of his stuff. He pounded away at the typewriter a while but pretty soon he got cold, not having much fur on him, and went out. I went out with him. Well, along the street he went, his head up in the clouds, and I was at his heels. Then I saw a dog. The dog got after me and I lit up a tree, a little one in the corner of the courthouse yard. It wasn't Pat Collins' dog. I don't know whose dog that was. I saw a lot of dogs while I was out on this party.

And so the dog went away and I got down out of the tree. Constable W. W. Farris picked me up. He petted me a while and was going to take me home with him. I wished he had. It would have saved me a bum night.

The constable took me down near the printshop and there were some young kids playing in the sand pile down by the machinery building—the beautiful one the boss gets sarcastic about sometimes. I guess the constable thought I belonged to the kids. He put me down. Night came.

A night of dogs, of bad dreams, of cold. It was Christmas Eve, too. I kept following people along streets. I mewed a lot. Every time I thought someone was going to take me home and feed me up, I saw another dog. Finally, I got so afraid and discouraged and hungry and cold I gave up and went into an old shed. Lordy, what a night. Bells ringing, too, people laughing. I never slept a wink.

And then morning came at last, Christmas morning. I tell you what, I'm a printshop cat. I can smell printer's ink a mile off. It was my instinct for printer's ink saved me, I'll tell you that.

I had come out of the shed and was standing in the street. I smelled something in the air, far off, so I trotted along a street.

Do you know what I smelled? It was Marvin Anderson. I understand he isn't a printshop man now, but he was once. I can spot them, all right. I can smell 'em, I tell you what.

So I trotted along and crawled through a fence and was in Mrs. E. H. Higginbotham's yard. My instincts had led me right. This Marvin Anderson married a Higginbotham girl. He has some fine children, all right. They picked me up and took me in the house. I got fed up fine. Christmas day went grand for me.

I guess Mr. Marvin Anderson's children thought I was a Christmas cat. They thought Santa Claus brought me but they were wrong about that. If Marvin Anderson had stayed in the printing business, I'd have stayed with his children.

He didn't; so Zeb came from the printshop and took me home. Thanks to Mrs. Higginbotham and the Anderson children for a fine Christmas dinner. I would have liked to stay with them but the paper has got to get out. They can't do a thing down at the printshop without me.

Folks of Marion, I'm home.

NELLIE THE CAT.

ATTEMPTED HOLDUP: Mr. John Dix
Manages to Escape

January 12

Another strange and startling experience on the highway. We are returning to the old days of desperate, cunning men. It is well to be on your guard.

Here is the latest highway story. Mr. John Dix, a prominent businessman of Pulaski, was spending the day in Marion. He is quite intimately connected with the life over here, being one of the directors of Marion College. After finishing his business in Marion, he started to drive home.

On the highway, just east of town, he saw what looked to be an old woman struggling along the road with a heavy grip in her hand.

Being a kind-hearted man, Mr. Dix stopped to pick her up.

They drove along in silence for some time and then something happened. Mr. Dix became suspicious of his passenger. He looked at her hands. They were not the hands of an old woman but of a young man.

Mr. Dix became convinced he was in the hands of a young outlaw. Everyone knows that in such a situation the driver of a car is in an ugly position. The very fact that he is driving makes him helpless.

In this position Mr. Dix resorted to a cunning plan to save himself. He leaned out of the car window and his hat blew off. He

pretended it was difficult for him to get out of the car and asked the
woman to get out and recover his hat. When she, or he, had got
out, Mr. Dix drove rapidly off.

Afterwards, it was found his suspicions were sound. The bag left
in the car by the old woman contained a set of burglar's tools. Mr.
Dix escaped luckily from a very risky person.

NELLIE IS DEAD: The Printshop Cat
Passes Away Quietly in a Shoe Box

January 12

The many friends of Nellie, the printshop cat, will be
grieved to hear of her death.

After returning from the escapade of Christmas Eve, when, if
you will remember, Nellie had to spend the night abroad in a cold,
empty shed, shaken by fear of dogs, hungry and miserable, Nellie
found a warm home and a good Christmas dinner in the home of
Mrs. E. H. Higginbotham and was later returned to her home in
the printshop, she seemed all right and quite happy.

For several days she was her old self. However, the terrible
experience through which she had passed had left its mark. Nellie
was as affectionate as ever but did not seem strong. After several
days she became really ill.

By the middle of last week her case was serious. Her disease was
diagnosed as pneumonia.

There is something terrible about seeing such a little animal
suffer. During the three days' illness before her death she never
complained. A shoe box had been provided for her and it had been
filled with soft white cloth.

For three days Nellie lay quietly in the box, refusing all food and
breathing with difficulty. Her little body shook with spasms of pain.

Jack, Gil, Joe, and Zeb went quietly about the shop with serious looks on their faces. It was rather odd to see a young fellow like Buck Fever so upset. He wouldn't go near the box to look at Nellie.

Nellie died on Friday, the 6th, at 2:09 in the afternoon. We were late with the *News* last week. It was just going to press.

Gil, who was feeding the paper into the press, got down off his pressman's stand and went to look at Nellie in her box. We all saw him put his hand down upon her. Then he looked at his watch. "She's dead," he said and went back to feeding the press. The machinery that had been stopped started again. There was a sharp little feeling of relief all through the shop. At least the little animal's hours of suffering were at an end.

It is a little odd, dear readers, to have so much fuss made about a cat.

Nellie was a tiny thing. She was never very strong. It will be easy enough to get another cat.

But it will be hard to find another cat that will be such a little bundle of affection as Nellie.

A BITTER PILL

January 19

This paper has just had a sad, sad experience. In last week's paper we thought we had achieved that most toothsome of all things to a newspaper, a clean "beat."

You know, when it comes to news, we weeklies are at a disadvantage compared to the dailies. As a matter of fact, we do not expect to be right down to the minute on "news."

We had stumbled upon what we thought a grand story about Mr. John Dix of Pulaski. Perhaps you read the story—how Mr. Dix picked up an old woman on the highway and looked at her hands. Then the coming of suspicion and how he cleverly let his hat blow out of the car window. After he had escaped, Mr. Dix had found, in a bag left in the car by the old woman, a set of burglar's tools.

A marvelous story, truly. The *Roanoke Times* handed us a bouquet: "Marion Paper Scores Clean Beat." O, sweet words. The editor of this paper loves to think of himself as essentially a modest man. When a thing of this sort happens he doesn't brag to anyone but his wife. Before his wife, when he is alone with her, he does throw out his chest. "My dear, did you see what I did? Did you see the *Roanoke Times* cracking me up as a newspaperman?"

O, sad, sad bereavement. The John Dix story wasn't true. Mr. Dix now says it never happened at all. Well, someone we trusted told us the story. This wail is partly addressed to our informant. O, Mr. C———, why did you betray our young faith? Did you make that story up or were you spoofing us?

And, Mr. Dix. Why did you not back us up? We never had a newspaper beat before. If it never happened to you on the highway, why did you not lie a little? Really, we had made you out as very clever, had we not? If you, Mr. Dix, had been running a newspaper beat, a small thing like the truth or falsehood of the story would never have stopped us. We would have lied for you to the limit.

Well, alas and alas—the story evidently was not true. Our only newspaper beat has vanished into thin, thin air.

ROMANCE ON THE HIGHWAY:
Was It the Wampus?

January 19

A dark and rainy night. Mayor Dickinson had come home and had got out his book. The Mayor is a great reader. He was in a soft easy chair. Outside it rained. Nothing nicer than sitting in an easy chair under a good light with a good book. The rain pounding on the roof overhead.

Suddenly the telephone rang. The mayor jumped up. Floating over the phone an alarmed voice.

A man who gave the name of Nelson was driving east along the highway toward Marion. At the overhead bridge three men, he said, jumped out and confronted him, demanding that he throw up his hands. For a moment, the man named Nelson said, he had hesitated and then had taken a chance. He had stepped on the gas and had managed to make a getaway.

Then he had gone to a nearby house and had phoned to our mayor. His voice trembled so he could scarcely speak.

Well, it was a bad night to go out but duty is duty. The mayor got out Sheriff Dillard and Jailor Hopkins and, getting into a car, they set out. They had decided to get themselves held up by the three desperate men. They rode up and down the highway for an hour. Not a soul in sight. The rain beat on the roof of the car. The mayor was thinking of his easy chair and his book.

Romance is all right, but when you go after it and do not get it! What a nice surprise for the highwayman had he or she or they or it tried to hold up that trio.

However, nothing happened. It was another John Dix romance. No doubt, some motorist got scared by his own shadow, or his own thoughts.

Three wet men coming back to town. No more sign of Nelson, no robbers. Anyway, we didn't get caught on that one. Jim Shanklin says it was the Wampus. He says the Wampus has been restless nights now for some time. Last night he says he went out to look in the Wampus cage and the Wampus was gone.

He is looking for this man Nelson's address. He is afraid the man has got away with the Wampus.

WINTER DAY IN THE COUNTRY

January 19

Extraordinary days, coming in the midst of winter. In town this writer was reminded of winter days in Mobile and New Orleans. But what a different country this from the low, swampy flatlands of the gulf states.

On Sunday to Wytheville by the highways and the afternoon spent exploring many side roads along the road, all aglow with soft, rich colors.

For every country its own prevailing color. Years ago I used to try to paint. I had never learned to draw but color always excited me. There are few enough people who see color, just as there are few people who hear sounds.

To be sure, obvious sounds are heard. You hear the scream of a railroad engine or a factory whistle. But what of the multitude of little sounds, overlaid one upon another, the sounds that come to the ear of a finely trained musician? Such a man would hear a hundred sounds that altogether escape our ears, would separate them just as a well-trained hunting dog separates scents.

To see color, the same training, the same care and absorption in the subject over a long period, is necessary. I never got very far with it.

Once when I was living for a winter on Mobile Bay I used to go in the afternoon and lie for hours on the beach, studying the shades of color in the bay, in the surrounding country, and in the sky. The bay absorbed something of color out of the sky, the sky out of the bay, and both borrowed from the land.

The land down there was red. Often at evening the sky and the bay both became blood-red.

In Grayson, where I have been living recently, the prevailing color is blue. It is almost the blue of the skies of Paris. There is the same clear light.

And we have the same extraordinary clear light here in Smyth. It is partly because of the altitude.

The land here is inclined toward a tawny yellow. Skies are often a clear, pale blue. The sky, lending its color to the land, produces a strange coppery landscape. It is always touched with spots of red and bright yellow.

This Southwest Virginia has always seemed to me an ideal painters' land, but if there has ever been a painter here I have never heard of him. I do not mean painters of flowers, mere daubers. Fine painters are rare. America has produced but a few of them. I mean a man in whom the sense of color is highly developed and who has that other rare thing, a quick sense of line.

To a painter of this sort the winter here would be even finer than the summer. In the winter, because our hills here are sharply outlined, the very bones of the country may be seen and felt.

And what a rich structure this Southwest Virginia has. How sensual all the lines here. Passing over into the Rich Valley, for example, on any of the roads I have been on over Walker's Mountain, in all the scene that rolls out before your eyes that combination of the sensual and the solid so often seen in old Italian paintings, done by the old masters.

People in general have an odd idea about the art of painting. They think it means merely getting down on canvas, very cleverly, a pretty picture. Well, it means much more than that.

There have been men in some countries—all of the great landscape painters have been like that—who have felt for some particular section of country much as a lover might feel for a woman he loved. He comes into the presence of a scene in the country he loves much in the spirit in which he might come into the presence of a beloved woman. His painting becomes, in fact, a form of making love.

There is something deeply stirred in him, purified. One of the painter Van Gogh's greatest paintings was of a single great sunflower in full bloom. When he made that particular painting he was so exhausted with the depth of his emotions that he was a sick man for days afterward. He hung the picture in his room. Gauguin, another great painter, came in and stood before it a moment. Then he shouted with a loud voice. In a moment he saw the marvelous thing the man had done.

And what is it that makes such a painting marvelous? At the core of it is love. In spite of all progress, all talk of progress and civilization, love remains the only truly powerful force in the world. The Christians have that clearly defined, although there are few enough men and women who call themselves Christians who would dare face the challenge back of their faith or who know much of love.

There is love of a particular thing. It might be just a sunflower. The same man, Van Gogh, a Dutchman, made one of his greatest paintings with his theme a kitchen chair. Today that little painting of a chair in a workingman's cottage is worth more even in money than the finest farm in all Southwest Virginia.

Why?

It takes a long time and training of the senses to know why. I sat for hours before the painting once. Gradually, as I sat there, I came to realize that the man who painted it had put into that simple painting a kind of wonder that as you look steals over your own senses. He had got the bones of what he felt, the delicate shades of color, the meaning. The man had felt something toward all other humans and had in that simple painting condensed the feeling of an entire lifetime.

But I am off the track again. I was talking of our own hills, the delicate colors to be seen here, the fine strength combined with softness in the turn of our hills. A drive into the country on a fine winter day—there is a treat never to be forgotten. Just now, at this season when the plow has been at work on some of the fields, turning up new earth, when the dead, burned grass of last year lies on meadow hillsides like tawny hair, when the clear streams reflect the soft pastel colors of our skies, there is a richness to the days that should make us all glad we live where we do.

WINTER DAY IN TOWN

January 19

Snow on the sidewalks, in the streets. The time of cold rains, cold winds. How nice the houses are now. The editor of this paper likes to walk in the streets alone at night. He goes down one street, crosses over, and goes along another. The houses are all lighted. There are fires burning.

People sitting in the houses—men, women, and children. Houses are like people. I beg you all when you walk thus, when your minds are not occupied with your own affairs, to begin thinking of houses.

The houses have faces. The windows are eyes. Some houses smile at you; others frown.

There are some houses that are always dark. People in them crawl off early to bed. You hear no laughter from such houses; no one sings.

Other houses are pretty proud. They are well-kept. As you pass, they seem to look at you with a sort of "keep off the grass" expression. You hurry past such houses.

I know houses that always seem to be whispering to me. There are secrets hidden in such houses. They plead with you not to disturb them. Alas, I am an inveterate hunter of tales. Odd things happen to people behind the walls of houses. Many people are one thing inside their houses and another on the street. Sometimes the secrets hidden away behind the walls of houses are merely sad, but sometimes they are exciting, too.

There are evenings when I walk thus and see houses that they all seem to be talking to me. They are trying to tell me what I cannot understand.

I go past a dozen houses, two dozen. There are the glad houses, the gay ones, the ones where all the doors seem ready to burst open. Some houses shout at me. "Come in," they say.

The man who loves life and people shows it in the way he walks along the street. His house would tell us his secret if we could only understand.

MYSTERIOUS CHECKER KING SHOWS MARION HIS CURVES

January 26

He came into town about the middle of last week, a rather quiet man with a little black mustache and a nervous step. Perhaps you know that Bill Johnson's shop, down facing the Marion-Rye Valley Railroad, is the checker center in Marion. There is a little room back in there, behind the shop, with a stove and a little table with its checker board.

For years now the checker tournaments of Marion have been fought out in that room. Perhaps Mr. Johnson himself is the champion among our players.

Others who are devotees of the game are Mr. James W. Sheffey, H. A. Stephenson, T. K. Sawyers, Ed Scott, Jess Hankla, and Bill Waterson. These men are all good players. No one of them can be dead sure of beating another.

And then this man named Ward came along; at least he said that was his name. He said he had once been a famous surgeon in a big New York hospital. It might have been true. Something had happened to the man all right. What it was no one knew.

He just wandered into the shop one day last week and asked if they played checkers there. They did. Someone asked him to sit into a game. He did.

A few moves and his opponent was whipped. It was hard to see how he did it. He seemed to have no special system. For all the jokes made about the game, checkers is about as complex a game as chess. There are a thousand combinations possible.

This man Ward seemingly knew them all. Sometimes he played a tight game and at other times opened wide up. He had our checker players woozy. No one in Marion ever saw such checkers. Word ran all over town, and all of the latter part of last week the checker headquarters of Marion was crowded. Then the mysterious checker king disappeared as mysteriously as he had come, but for years the men who loved checkers will be talking of his game and wishing he had stayed long enough to give them a real chance to get onto his curves.

MR. GROUND HOG: Groundhogging

February 2

We don't care. He can see his shadow if he wants to. It's all right with us.

Well, he was out and saw it early—a nice, big, black shadow. I suppose people who have lived here a long time call what we have been having here recently "winter." We don't call it that. We lived once in Chicago.

Mild, soft mornings. From the window of our room, we see over the roofs of the town into the hills. The morning air is clear and sharp. If this be winter, give us more of it.

Last year a too-early spring played the deuce with all of our fruit. The ground hog has been much maligned. He is really the friend of humanity. Given a chance to see his shadow, he lays the blanket of winter over the earth until it is really time for spring.

Which makes me think—over in Grayson they kill and eat ground hogs. It always seemed too bad to me. If there ever was a harmless little beast, that one is. He usually lives somewhere along the bank of a small stream. He is a clean little thing and likes green things and fruits. When I was a boy I was very fond of fishing. I used to go lie on the bank of a small stream near our town. I didn't fish much, just lay there for hours dreaming. There was a ground hog lived in the stream near where I frequently went. After a while he got used to my presence.

He used to come down to the bank of the stream and sit there on his haunches and look at me. No one ever shot or hunted ground hogs about there, and they were very tame. There were berry bushes at the edge of the field where he lived and he would start picking berries. He sat up on his hind legs, reached up and got ahold of the bushes, and pulled them down until he could reach the berries. He seemed very happy and contented with life, as all wild animals do when you let them alone.

IN WASHINGTON

February 9

In Washington, where I have been sent to interview the Secretary of Commerce, Mr. Hoover. I do not like the job much. Why did I take it?

I am always undertaking something the Lord never intended me to do.

I have arrived in the city in the early morning and am not to see the man until late afternoon. It is bitter cold. When I saw Washington last, some fifteen or twenty years ago, it was merely a great, struggling town. Now it has become a modern city.

I have been at a big hotel and have left my bag. I begin wondering what I shall do with my day.

We who live in country towns miss certain things. The radio and the phonograph can bring us music by the best orchestras (if there are any bests), we can hear speakers talk, but there are things we cannot get.

We cannot see the best players on the stage and we cannot see paintings.

I decided to go to a museum.

There are days for everything. Was this a day to see paintings? I should, no doubt, have gone to talk to some politician but I knew no politicians as politicians. No one ever talks politics to me. I went to the new Freer Gallery.

The Freer Gallery was built by a rich man of Detroit and was intended primarily to house the paintings of the American painter Whistler. It is called "The Freer Gallery" for its builder. In it are housed most of the more famous paintings of James McNeill Whistler and, in addition to these, many old and rare objects of Chinese and Japanese art.

I went to the gallery in the morning and it was quite empty but for the attendants. There was a hushed quiet over the place. The walls and the attendants seemed crying out at me, "Be careful, walk quietly, this is a sacred place."

Sacred, indeed. What a strange thing is the life of the artist.

Standing in the gallery and looking at these paintings, conscious all the time of the uniformed attendants watching me, afraid perhaps I might steal some of these sacred objects, an odd feeling of annoyance creeping over me.

Such a man as Whistler lives. His work is condemned or praised by the men of his own time. It has been the fate of some men who have produced the greatest art, made the greatest discoveries in science, the greatest contributions to scholarship, to live and die unknown. They are perhaps the lucky men.

Such a man as Whistler, fighting for fame. He was always a great fighter. Once he wrote a book called *The Gentle Art of Making Enemies*. He knew how to do that, all right.

Much of his energy must have been spent in fighting for fame. Well, he has won. He has fame. Fame, in the end, does not always mean worth. If you keep insisting that you are a great man, after a time people will believe. It doesn't necessarily mean you are great.

James McNeill Whistler was not one of the great painters of the world. His fighting and his personality got him somewhere. A rich patron of the arts, Mr. Freer, became devoted to him. He has spent hundreds of thousands of dollars, his time, his own energy, in making Mr. Whistler's fame secure. Mr. Freer, because of his devotion to another, may possibly be a finer and a greater man than Mr. Whistler.

As for myself, I could not get over the feeling that much of Mr. Whistler's work is vastly overestimated. Many of these paintings hung over by paid attendants, housed in this great stone building, are commonplace enough.

I went out of the famous Peacock Room and into the room where the older art treasures are housed. There were the old Chinese and Japanese things.

Objects of art come out of a day when there was no such thing as publicity—paintings by reticent, devoted men. Whistler has been rather widely advertised as having brought over into his own day much of the fineness of these older painters. He has not brought over so much.

Such a short time ago, some fifty years, and Whistler's house in London was being sold over his head. Many of these paintings, so sumptuously housed now, were sold then for a few shillings. Have they increased in value so much?

The value of the older Chinese and Japanese things is fixed. Money cannot express it. There is "The Waves at Matsushinea," painted by some unknown man called "Satatsu" in the seventeenth century. In another painting the Chinese Emperor Ming Huang is with his concubine Kuei-fei in a garden. What a charming lady! It is spring. She is singing to make the flowers bloom for her emperor.

And there is another painting. The Emperor Weu, of the Chou Dynasty, is meeting the sage, Chiang Tzu-ya. The two men are meeting on an island in a winding lake. All nature seems hushed and quiet. Clouds are standing still in the sky, as though intent on the scene below. There is a sense in the painting of infinite time, space, distance.

Mr. Hoover and I did not meet on an island in a winding lake. There were no fleecy clouds floating in the sky, no sense of infinite time, space, distance.

It may be that Mr. Hoover has in him the making of an emperor, but I am no sage.

If I had been a sage I would not have been where I was.

I was in a great office building in the modern city of Washington. Before me sat a well-dressed man of perhaps fifty. Like myself, he was a bit too fat. He had leaned too long over a desk, over figures and plans; and I had leaned too long over a typewriter. Besides that, Mr. Hoover had just been to a dentist.

And he did not want to be interviewed.

"Are you an interviewer?" he asked. "Yes," I said doubtfully. I had never been such a thing before. I am a writer of books, sometimes a teller of tales. I run a country weekly. Country weeklies are not newspapers. We do not interview people. I am not a politically minded man. Always I am asking myself the question, "Why does anyone want to be president? Why does any man want power?"

By my philosophy, power is the forerunner of corruption.

To be a bright, intelligent newspaper interviewer, I should have asked Mr. Hoover some embarrassing questions. He was a member of the cabinet of Mr. Harding, sat cheek by jowl with Mr. Fall and Mr. Daugherty. A stench arose from that sitting.* What about it?

The question trembled on my lips.

Other questions crowding into my mind. "What of the League of Nations, our attitude toward the small republics of Central America?"

Better that I should not ask such questions. The man would twist me about his little finger. "It is just possible he knows something about leagues of nations and all such things, but what do you know?" I was now asking myself.

A fragment of song floated up into my mind, even then, at that unfortunate moment. The song was like the clouds floating above that island when the Emperor Weu went to meet Chiang Tzu-ya.

"My freedom sleeps in a mulberry bush.

---

* Albert Bacon Fall (1861–1944) and Harry Micajah Daugherty (1860–1941) served respectively as President Warren G. Harding's Secretary of the Interior and Attorney General until the Teapot Dome oil scandal caused them to resign in 1923 and 1924. Fall was convicted of bribery in 1929 and served a prison term in 1931–32. Daugherty was acquitted in 1929 of a charge of conspiracy to defraud the federal government.

"My country is in the shivering legs of a little, lost dog."

"I am not going to be interviewed," Mr. Hoover said again. "I don't care," I said. As a matter of fact, I did not care two straws. I had made a futile trip to Washington. Well, it was not futile. I had seen the Emperor Ming Huang with his concubine Kuei-fei walking in a garden.

The Emperor Ming Huang had walked in his garden with Kuei-fei in another age than my own. There were no factories in that age. Men did not rush through the streets in automobiles. There were no radios, no airplanes.

Just the same, men fought wars; men were cruel and greedy, as in my own age.

My mind full of things far removed from Mr. Hoover and his age. I was going out the door, having got nothing from him, having failed as a modern newspaper correspondent—a task that no such man as myself should have undertaken—when Mr. Hoover called me back.

"I will not be interviewed, but we can talk," he said. Mr. Hoover was being kind. He must have felt my incompetence. I understood what he meant. He meant only that things were to be in his own hands. We were to speak only of those things that Mr. Hoover cared to discuss.

He began to talk now, first of the Mississippi problem. It was a huge problem, he said, but it could be met. There was a way out.

There was the river cutting down through the heart of the country, twisting and winding. Had I not spent days and weeks on the great river? I told him I had. "It is uncontrollable," I said. "The Mississippi is a thing in nature. It is nature." But did not Joshua make the sun stand still? I remembered a summer when I took the Mississippi as a god, became a river worshipper.

I was in a boat fishing on the Mississippi when a flood came. I felt its power; it put the fear of God into my heart.

But Mr. Hoover had been down there and was not afraid. He spoke of spillways. There was to be a new river bed creeping down westward of the Mississippi—all through the lower country.

Then when great floods came rampaging and tearing down and Mother Mississippi was on the rampage, she was to be split in two.

Two Mother Mississippis, gentled now, going down to the sea. "What a man," I said to myself.

And could he also handle like that the industrial age?

There was the question. That also had become to me like a thing in nature.

I had, after all, got down to the heart of what I wanted to ask Mr. Hoover.

The industrial age has been sweeping forward ever since I was a boy. I have seen the river of it swell and swell. It has swept over the entire land. The industrialists may not be Ming Huangs, but they are in power.

They have raised this Mr. Hoover up out of the ranks of men as perhaps the finest Republican example of manhood and ability in present-day American political and industrial life. He is, apparently, a man very sure of himself. His career has been a notable one. From a small beginning, he has risen steadily in power. There has never been any check. I felt, looking at him, that he has never known failure.

It is too bad never to have known that. Never to have known miserable nights of remorse, feeling the world too big and strange and difficult for you.

Well, power also, when it is sure of itself, can gentle a man. Mr. Hoover has nice eyes, a clear, cool voice. He gave me long rows of figures showing how the industrialists have improved things for the common man. We spoke of Mr. Ford, and he was high in his praise of the man. "When I go to ride in an automobile," he said, "It does not matter to me that there are a million automobiles on the road just like mine. I am going somewhere and want to get there in what comfort I can and at the lowest cost."

That, it seemed to me, summed up Mr. Hoover's philosophy of life.

When you have a man's philosophy of life, why stay about? Why bother the man?

Mr. Hoover spoke of the farmers. It is quite true that, in the distribution of the good things the industrial age has brought, the industrialists and the financiers have got rather the best of it. Labor has been able to take good care of itself, Mr. Hoover thinks. The farmer is another problem. Here is one place where the modern system has not quite worked.

It is a matter, he said, of too much waste between the farmer and the consumer. I gathered that the whole system of merchandising would have to be brought up into the new age.

"Something like the systems of chain stores," I suggested. He fended me off there. I presume any man in political life has to be cautious. The merchant class is a large class. There are votes there. My mind flopped back to my own town. Voters gathered in the evening at the back of the drugstore, the hardware store, the grocery store. The small, individual merchant who is, I gather, at the bottom of the farmer's troubles, has power too—in his own store.

There has been something hanging in my mind for a long time. I thought I would at least take a shot at it. All of this industrialism and standardization growing up in my day. I had seen it grow and grow. A whole nation riding in the same kind of cars, smoking the same kind of cigars, wearing the same kind of clothes, thinking the same thoughts.

Individualism among the masses of the people gradually dying.

You get a few men, drawn up and become powerful because they control the mass needs and the mass thought. No questions asked any more. All doubting men thrown aside.

Young men, buried yet down in the mass, squirming about. They not liking too well the harness of industrialism and standardization. Men coming into power, not as Lincoln came, nor yet as Napoleon came.

At the bottom of it all a growing number of the younger men feeling hopeless boredom.

Is the heavy boredom of a standardized civilization true for Mr. Hoover, as it is sometimes true for me? I asked Mr. Hoover that question and for the first time during our talk he did not seem comfortable.

But power is power. He fended off again. After all, the age and the system of the age that may destroy one man may make another. Mr. Hoover has been made by his age. Apparently, he is satisfied with it.

I got out of Mr. Hoover's presence feeling we had got nowhere.

Surely it wasn't his fault. I went walking for a long time in the streets of Washington. The more I walked the more sure I was that Mr. Hoover is the ideal among Republican men to be the present-day president of the United States—if he can make them see it.

Other men feel that. I asked several, men I had never seen before.

I asked a man who drove a streetcar, one who opened oysters, another who scrubbed the floor in the lobby of a hotel.

"He is the ideal man," they all said. They were afraid the politicians would not give him the chance. The reason given was that he has too much brains.

But these men's opinion has also been made by the standardized newspaper opinion of the age in which they live. Their expression of doubt was merely resentment. Mr. Hoover is the blameless man. In Mr. Hoover's head has developed the ideal brain for his time. Are the other leaders of his party afraid of him? Surely theirs are not the nameless fears of such men as myself.

It would be a little odd if, the age having produced a perfect thing, a man who does so very well and with such fine spirit just what everyone apparently believes they want done—should be thrown aside, being too perfect.

There is no doubt in my own mind. I am convinced Mr. Hoover would make the ideal Republican president.

No one will ever sing songs about Mr. Hoover after he is president—if they decide to give him the chance. There will be no paintings made of him walking at evening in a garden while a lovely lady sings to make the flowers bloom.

But it is not an age of painting, not an age of song.

And so there was I walking in the streets of Washington, having made a failure of my day. I had tried to be smart and had not been smart. I had got myself into a false position. What happens to the age in which a man lives is like the Mississippi, a thing in nature. It is no good quarreling with the age in which you live.

I had come to Washington, I think, wanting to like Mr. Hoover and had ended by admiring him. He had not warmed me. I went over past the White House and tried to think of Lincoln living there. Then I went back to the Freer Gallery for another look at Ming Huang walking in his garden and listening to the voice of Kuei-fei—but it was closed for the night.

WHAT IS VULGARITY?

February 9

Would we all prefer to retain the innocence of childhood? It can't well be done but would it be better if we could do it?

To attempt to meet life a little boldly, to admit to yourself that a spade is a spade, is a challenge.

Is it vulgar to really look a little at life, to try to see and understand it a little as it is?

Many people prefer what is called among writers "the ivory tower." You live in the ivory tower when you shut yourself off from facts. You make yourself believe what you like to believe. Many people go on like that most of their lives. It is one way of life. They try to escape all of the vulgarities of life by ignoring them.

Many things cannot be completely ignored—birth, death, disease, passions, lusts. Lusts, for example, too much suppressed, lead to all sorts of insanities.

There are many people who are compelled by their work to lose a certain delicate attitude toward life. What about the doctor, for example? The doctor would be a very poor doctor if he believed the stories about the nature of human life told within the walls of the ivory tower.

All men in direct contact with life get finally a certain balance or they go insane. It may be that true vulgarity lies in too much fear of the so-called "vulgar." Many of the vulgar facts of life, frankly accepted, cease to be vulgar.

Real vulgarity, like fineness, is an inner thing. The most vulgar people may be those who most pride themselves on their refinement.

JAMES OVERBAY GOES BACK

February 9

James Overbay, who has been at the reform farm and who has recently been out on a furlough, is going back. If you will remember, Sheriff Dillard went out to the Overbay place some time ago and found a still there. Jim DeBord was with him. This was early on a Sunday morning. The still was all ready to operate, the mash all there and everything. The nearest house is the Overbay house. It is surrounded by woods.

And so there sat the sheriff and Jim DeBord in the stillhouse, waiting for someone to come. Three very small children came up the path through the woods. They were the younger Overbay children, all little fellows. One of them had a small pail in his hand. Evidently, they were coming directly to the stillhouse, but one of the little fellows had sharp eyes. Through a crack he saw the sheriff sitting in there. That was the little chap that was carrying the pail. His mother says he was going to water a calf. No reflections on anyone.

Anyway, the little chap ran and the other children surrendered. There was the sound of someone else cutting out through the woods and there is a suspicion that it was James Overbay but there isn't any definite proof. He was to have gone on trial, defended by Mr. Bill Birchfield, but decided to go back to the reform farm instead. No reflection on Bill either.

So there wasn't any trial. Justice Dickinson gave the younger children a fatherly talk about walking toward stillhouses when they went for Sunday morning walks and that was that. BUCK.

CHILHOWIE'S BIG NIGHT

February 23

In the first place Mr. Charles Mercer got some whiskey. He says he got it from Lansing Nelkirk, sometimes called "Trip." He tripped that time, all right. Mr. Mercer says he got the whiskey from Trip and Trip admits it. As everyone knows, when Mr. Mercer has a few drinks in him, he is likely to get a bit rambumptious. This time he went home and began to tear up things. He burned up his shoes, broke his glasses, stamped on them, then chased Mrs. Mercer down the road.

It was a lively time for Mr. Beattie, Mayor of Chilhowie, too. This, as everyone knows, is lambing time. The mayor is a great sheep man. These February nights a man has to sit up with the mother sheep. Very little rest for him.

The sheep lambing and Mr. Mercer on the rampage. Chilhowie has had quieter nights.

CHAPTER TWO

And, while all of this was going on, where was Si Price, the town marshal? As we novelists love to say, he was off about other business in the quiet night.

John E. Hough and Robert Bobbett, it seems, had been accused of stealing some twenty-three hens from the Walker farm, near Chilhowie. Si had got Robert Bobbett and had got him lodged in the jail at Marion. Then he went after John Hough. He got on the trail Hough lit out. He is a good footer but so is Si. The night winds whistling through Si's hair. Who says there isn't plenty of good stuff for novelists in good old Smyth?

The trouble was that Bobby Robert—or, I should say, Robert Bobbett—lit out. It was a cold night. The river was deep.

The two men plunged down a steep bank. When they had got to the river's edge Si put out his hand to get hold of Hough's coat collar.

He had Bobbett and he just missed Hough. Into the stream plunged Hough. Si didn't follow. He says the night was too cold and that he would rather pay for the hens.

What he did was to stand on the shore and shake his fist at Hough. "Woof, woof, woof," cried Hough. The water was icy cold. Mr. Hough escaped and at this writing is still at large. We may be sure he had a cold night.

CHAPTER THREE

Scene: Mayor Beattie's court at Chilhowie. In the court-room Mr. Mercer and Mrs. Mercer, Si Price, Sheriff Dillard, your correspondent, Mr. Funk with his new haircut, Mr. Will Asbury. Crowds of curious standing about outside. Some suspicious-looking bottles on a table. We all smell the bottles. Mr. Trip Nelkirk says he got the stuff Mr. Mercer drank and that started him burning shoes from Charles Brooks, recently from Grayson but now living near the Red Bridge. I'll say this: if it tasted like it smells and Trip drank as much of it himself as he says he did, he is a hardy young man, all right.

CHAPTER FOUR

A tense moment. Mr. Trip did not want to tell. He wavered. Should he or should he not? He turned a bit pale and made nervous movements with his fingers. Then he went outside with county attorney Funk and they talked out there. Your correspondent, Si Price, and Sheriff Dillard spoke together of whether or not a man should plunge into a river on an icy night after a man accused of chicken stealing. The vote was two to one against Si, but then we were sitting in a warm room when we made our decision.

CHAPTER FIVE

Mr. Trip has decided not to tell. He comes back into the room and takes his seat. "Are you ready?" asks Mayor Beattie. "No," says Mr. Trip. "Ninety days and $50," says Mayor Beattie.

BOOK TWO

In the meantime a warrant had been sworn out for Mr. Charles Brooks, who owns a farm up the Comers Creek Road on top of Iron Mountain over in Grayson, but who, like your correspondent, is spending his winter in Smyth, Smyth being one of the finest winter resorts we have ever spent a winter in. Mr. Charles Brooks is the grandson of a famous old bear hunter named Brooks. The Brookses are fine people. He said he never sold any liquor to Mr. Trip Nelkirk—swears he never saw the man before. Mr. Charles Brooks was brought into Justice Farris' court in Marion and bound over to the grand jury in the sum of one thousand dollars. Bonds were furnished.

CHILHOWIE IS QUIET NOW

During all this excitement in Chilhowie, your correspondent got into a conversation with Mr. Beattie about sheep raising and the difficulties of the lambing time. If there is one thing in this world we love it is visiting a good, well-kept farm in lambing, in sheep shearing, or at the harvest. Having got into a conversation with Mr. Beattie about his lambs, we could not rest until we saw them; so in the late afternoon, after all this excitement, we drove to Chilhowie again to see the lambs fed in the evening.

A delightful evening with a soft mist floating over the hills. A fine, well-kept farm, good barns, stock all well cared for, the kind of farm we like and the kind of people we like.

It takes all kinds of experiences to make a newspaper day, but there are few enough of them that end so delightfully.

DAYS

March 1

My spirit is as heavy as lead. Such days come and go. Life is none too long. Good resolutions made. They slip away like the days. Criminals and so-called "good people." Where do we all stand?

What has killed the day for me? It has grown dark and gloomy. People hurry past me on the street. I have determined to make a newspaper but there are so many things to be put in a newspaper I do not want to put in.

There is a young boy accused of forging a check. I am walking along Main Street and see suddenly a flurry on the courthouse yard. The check was issued by a businessman of Marion. He gave it to a young girl who worked in his kitchen. The check disappeared.

It appeared next in a Marion store. The boy has apparently forged the girl's name on the back of the check and has got the money on it.

Now the boy is sitting with a pair of handcuffs on his wrists. He is frightened. His mother has gone into a sort of hysterics. She runs anxiously about, shouts, makes threats. She is like mother birds I have seen in the woods, their young threatened.

On her face traces of beauty. She was a handsome young woman, is still handsome.

She has a daughter, also handsome. I am depressed to see this family in trouble.

With the court officials I am forever having an argument. Is it better to be lenient, let offenders go? I am forever on the side of the man who has committed a crime. Surely society has to be protected.

No doubt, I am all wrong. I would never do to be any kind of a public officer.

There are some boys, sons of respectables, in trouble. Really they are young men. They went and got drunk and made a row on Main

Street. It was at night. Everyone apparently knows who they were but there was no positive proof. They are sticking to each other. Apparently, all the possible witnesses were their friends. Their friends will not appear against them.

They are anxious about me because they do not want their names put in the paper. I do not want to put their names in the paper; but last week, when some son of a workingman was in trouble, his name went in as a part of the police court news.

I do not want to put anyone's name in the paper in a way that will bring disgrace upon them; but I have at least, in a small way, undertaken the obligation of a newspaperman.

Too many country weeklies have been milk-and-water things. No news, no taking account of the march of everyday life in a town.

The three young men look at me with fright in their eyes. I do not like that. When I was a young man I was not such an angel. I am no angel yet.

Still, I am running a newspaper. I have undertaken the obligation of that job. When one of the young men has done something of which he can be proud, he will be proud to see it in the paper.

I am depressed because there seems an outburst of juvenile crime. What is the explanation of that?

In Saltville three boys have been robbing houses. Doctor Brown's house has been robbed and the houses of H. T. Spraker, J. L. Mullins, E. N. Bunts, and J. S. Nye.

The three boys were crafty. They robbed house after house. When they did not find money they took nothing. At one place they took thirty dollars, at another a dollar and a quarter. They took various small sums.

Their method was to have one of the boys go to a weekly prayer meeting at one of the churches. He watched to see who came in. Then the word was passed to the other two boys outside. One of the boys stayed on watch. If the man whose house was being searched for money left the church, he could cut out ahead of him and give warning.

Now they are caught and have confessed. The people who have been robbed agree to let them off this time. What will the judge decide?

If they are let off, will they be back in court in a few months, having committed other robberies?

What is the meaning of all this juvenile crime, getting drunk, etc.? It must be that there is some lack of interest in life. Cannot these boys find work that will interest them?

It is very well to blame the boys but there is a hole somewhere.

Life ought to be a dancing thing. It should be fun. Half the crime and so-called "bad behavior" in the world must come from boredom.

When I walk into the jail I cannot see any difference between the boys and men in there and those on the street. I cannot see any difference between them and myself.

I am depressed because life cannot be more decent and wholesome.

Days when every man speaks to another in an ugly way. There are times of mutual suspicion, greediness, lusts. Passions seem at times to sweep through all people; ugliness comes over people like a wind blowing.

Other days when there is a kind of gladness in the air. It affects all people. All people step with a livelier step. They greet each other with a smile.

It may be that crime and all bad behavior come from inner resentment that the relationships between all people cannot be carried on a bit higher and finer plane.

CATS—AND OTHER THINGS

March 1

We have a new cat. Mack Morris sent her to the shop. It is a very interesting thing about pets. There was Nellie, for example. You will remember that Nellie died. It is just possible that Nellie a little exhausted the store of affection of Zeb, Jack, Gil, Joe, and the rest of us.

I am talking to men now. Do you remember, when you were a boy, your first love? Mine was a red-haired girl. As I remember it, I never did speak to her.

At that time I was living in a town about the size of Marion. I had a job driving a delivery wagon for a grocer. I might have been thirteen or fourteen.

One day I was driving along the street and saw this red-haired girl. How unspeakably dainty she seemed to me. It seemed to me that my heart stopped beating.

Well, she breathed, she ate food, she lived in a house. Alas, her father was not in such an inspiring position in life. In that day, towns like Marion still had saloons. Her father was a bartender.

They lived in a little frame house on a certain street. To get to the end of that street and pass her house I had to go to the end of the street and turn. It was a cul-de-sac. How I wished our store had more trade on the street. As I remember it, we had none.

I was driving, to the grocery wagon, an old black horse. Poor old thing. A dozen times a day I drove her to the end of the street and turned. Other boys laughed at me. They knew, all right.

O, the suffering of the young heart!

That red-haired girl knew, too. Sometimes she let me see her. Sometimes she did not. She used to come out and stand on the porch of the house and pretend not to see me. I never did get courage to speak to her. When she spoke to me my cheeks burned with blushes.

It is a bit odd about women. We strong men are inclined to like and even love weak-looking women. Let a woman be too big, too strong and broad-shouldered, and we turn from her.

It is because weak, dainty-looking women make us feel strong and commanding.

What a joke life is. The weak, gentle-looking women so often bully us men a thousand times more than strong, healthy women ever would.

We fall for them just the same.

But we were speaking of cats. Nellie, our first Marion cat love, is dead. She has gone to her reward. The new cat is a handsome lady, as strong as Nellie was weak. She is a true cat with at least nine lives.

She is very affectionate, too. But look you now. She hasn't even a name. Won't some big, strong woman among our subscribers who has in her heart a secret sympathy with this new lady cat, knowing her strong, as I have said, an independent, fine, spirited cat, knowing the disadvantage she is under, following Nellie. . . .

Won't some such woman send in a name for the new lady cat? No need to reveal yourself. Send it on a postcard. You don't even need sign your name.

Do this as a rebuke to the men in the shop who love the weak rather than the strong.

TOM GREER

March 8

A slow-speaking, sensible man with a thousand friends. He loves wit and has a keen sense of humor. Men respect him for his solidity. When he tells you something, you believe it.

His business is one of the most interesting in town.

As a businessman, "Tom" Greer, Riley Thomas Greer, to be exact, reminds one more of a European businessman than an American. The modern American idea of "bigness" at any cost has not caught him. He is in business now with the same associates that have been with him almost from the beginning. The business is not a corporation but a partnership, and associated with Mr. Greer in the business is his cousin, George W. Greer, who conducts a branch of the business at Pikeville, Kentucky, and Mr. C. C. Stafford of Kentucky.

To a writing man there is a touch of romance to the business of dealing in roots, herbs, and barks. Walking through Mr. Greer's big warehouses, where there are bales of goods on all sides and, here and there, spread out on the floor to dry, fragrant roots, barks, and herbs, there floats through the mind visions of high mountain valleys, lonely spots along mountain streams, dense mountain forests.

Mr. Greer is a dealer in roots, herbs, and barks, the largest dealer perhaps in the country. Products from his warehouse go to cities all over the world.

Here are some of them: Virginia snakeroot, stillingia root, senega snakeroot, slippery elm bark (well rossed), shonny haw bark.

One hundred and fifty such items on the list of Mr. Greer's price lists. Who would not be a stillingia if they could, and well rossed, too?

Or a shonny haw?

Well do we remember the last time we were well rossed. What a headache we had! But that is neither here nor anywhere else.

Would you know any of these things if you saw them in the forest? Would you know a pipsissewa? How about a bugleweed herb?

People do know them, mountain people, women and boys.

Tom Greer was a boy over in Watauga County, North Carolina. His parents did not have any more money than we have now. As a boy he used to go around gathering shonny haw and pipsissewa. He sold it to a little country store six miles away.

In that country, at that time, they had school only three months a year and then the schoolhouse burned down. Tom Greer missed most of the disadvantages of modern education.

No one ever told him that he was anything special or that Italy lay over the Alps, and so he grew up to be the nice, quiet man we all know.

It was, from all accounts, a rather hard growing-up. There he was, with Marion, Virginia, the nearest railroad station, sixty-five miles north. He went to work in a country store. Already he knew the practical side of gathering roots and herbs, and now he learned something about the commercial side. He had got together two or three hundred dollars. You know how that boy had to work and save and go without to get that.

He had, however, got something else, too. There was a little company formed—Tom Greer, his cousin George, and two or three others, all mountain men. He had got the confidence of his neighbors.

They sent Tom and his cousin George out to scout the land. Tom landed in Marion and his cousin George at Pikeville, Kentucky. They were both the same kind of men. When they had made up their minds, they had made up their minds.

And so they went back and got their families and came out to the railroad in covered wagons, Tom to Marion and his cousin on to Pikeville.

Tom Greer began business here in a small way—very, very small, in fact. He had to teach the mountain people in the hills about Marion the medicinal roots and herbs. Many of them he gathered himself. There was little or no money. Mrs. Greer helped. In fact, Mrs. Greer has become an expert in certain branches of the business now.

Besides roots, herbs, and barks, pollen is now used in some of the modern treatments of diseases such as hay fever and asthma.

Pollen is gathered from the blossoms of all sorts of weeds, flowers, and grasses. It is delicate, particular business and must be done by an expert. This has become Mrs. Greer's line.

And in the meantime, all over the hills, people—largely women—go out into the woods to gather the medicinal herbs and barks that are sent into the Greer warehouse and prepared for shipment. The growth of the business has been slow but sure. From a few thousand dollars a year, it has grown so that there is now annually shipped from a quarter to a half million dollars' worth of goods.

The business is run as it was first started. When it was new and at a period of financial stress, Mr. Charles C. Stafford, a well-to-do farmer from near Pikeville, Kentucky, put into the business some six thousand as additional working capital and did it against the advice of his banker and merely because he liked the looks of Tom Greer and his cousin George.

For that little act of generosity and keen judgment of human nature, Mr. Stafford has been getting back each year about the full amount he put in and has been getting it for many years. There have been years when he got two or three times that much.

As I said at the beginning, Mr. Tom Greer is like a good many

European businessmen. Many temptations have come to him to spread out, to spread-eagle, to plunge into this or that. However, they have really not been temptations at all.

Mr. Greer has always been interested in his own business. He likes it, never loses interest. Today he is the same quiet, unassuming man he was when he came to Marion—some say, laughingly—barefooted out of the hills. He is a man going about his affairs quietly and efficiently, rolling a bit of wit under his tongue, enjoying his town, his neighbors, and the business in which he has been so successful.

OLD CHEW

March 22

One of the most distinctive characters of our town is Dr. Thompson's big old black dog "Chew." Chew has grown rather heavy now. He has become a gourmand. Daily he goes his rounds.

He appears at the door of Hall's restaurant. If no one pays any attention to him, he scratches on the door until someone admits him. There is food to be had there. He knows that.

Another favorite place of call is Bill Johnson's meat market. In the morning, often, he goes to meet Mr. Johnson coming to his shop. He has perhaps been abstemious all night. He capers and bounces in the road about Mr. Johnson and follows him to his shop. Well, he is seldom disappointed. When he gets his bit of meat, he goes away, wagging his tail.

In the same way, he has made friends with Mr. Roscoe Pruner.

There are pickings to be had there, too. He gets a bone or a piece of meat and goes contentedly over into the courthouse yard.

A half dozen places of call and all good ones. No wonder he is fat.

When he was a younger dog, he once did a fine deed. Dr.

Thompson's children were sliding down the hill opposite his house. At the bottom of the hill it is necessary to give a sled a sharp turn. There is a steep bank there and a barb-wire fence. The youngest child was sliding down the hill and did not make the turn. He was headed for the bank, with a bad fall and injury not unlikely, when old Chew, seeing his predicament, rushed at him and threw him off the sled into the snow.

As I have suggested, nowadays Chew has grown fat. He walks sedately along the street. If you do not run a restaurant, a hotel, or a meat market, he will pay no attention to you. He knows what he knows.

SNOWY NIGHTS

April 5

I don't so often wish I were rich but sometimes I do. I am always seeing things I want. A fast red automobile, a grand house to live in. I would like a string of running horses. Also, I would keep a few fast trotters and pacers.

I would like to wear silks. Once I had a grand idea. You know how the performers dress at the grand opera in the cities—kingly robes. I thought I would go and get me a lot of second-hand kingly robes and wear them around. Wouldn't I look grand going down Marion's Main Street in a kingly robe? O, boy.

If I could only have remained always about thirty-three or four. A lot of people talk of being tired of life. I am not tired of it. It makes me sick to think I can't go banging about for the next three hundred years.

Watching the show—watching the wheels go round.

You know that Negro song, "There is a wheel within a wheel, away up yonder in the sky."

I like to walk around trying to think why people do as they do, why some are what is called "good" and others what is called "bad."

On Sunday night, the 17th of March, year of our Lord 1928. The town was very quiet and still. It had been snowing all day and all the night before.

The snow began with a rain, wetting everything thoroughly, so that the snow, when it came, all stuck.

It was still snowing when I set out from my house. The world was white.

In my mind a line, just snatched out of a book of fine poems I had been reading. The book by Miss Marjorie Meeker of Columbus, Ohio.*

"This wary winter that was white so long."

Winter of life, eh?

"This wary winter that was white so long."

I kept saying the words over to myself as I walked, loving them.

Loving, too, the memory I had of the woman who wrote the lines. I saw her once sitting in her big, fine house.

Everyone who lives here knows how white and beautiful that Sunday night was in Marion, Virginia.

I walked out Main Street to where the houses end to the east and then back again, through town, to where they end at the west.

It may have been rather late. There was no one abroad. When I had got out west of town, I climbed over a fence into a field.

A few people driving closed cars on the highway. The lights of the cars were nice, playing over the fields and among the branches of trees.

Every limb and twig of the trees outlined in white.

I wishing suddenly and crazily for a horse to ride, a white, clean-limbed, galloping horse. Thinking of that old man Ryder's galloping horse in the mysterious night. Have you ever seen that painting?

"This wary winter that was white so long."

A white horse, galloping across fields, in and out of white forests.

Or a sleigh with a fine team of trotters or pacers hitched to it, eh?

Such a team as I once drove but never owned. Fiery boys they were.

* From "This Wary Winter," *Color of Water* (New York: Brentano's, 1928), p. 33.

"Ripshin," Sherwood Anderson's Country Home in Grayson County, Virginia

Anderson's Study at "Ripshin"

I was working for their owner then—a mere groom—not a proud editor as I am now. Alas, you see, there is no aristocratic blood in me.

Once, on just such another wonder night as that of last Sunday, the owner of that team was away from home. In the barn there was a sleigh with white swans' heads thrust out in front.

I was in love with a little country girl just at that time.

And so, on that night, I stole the team and the sleigh out of the barn, not putting on the sleigh bells, not wanting anyone to hear and tell my boss.

Fiery blacks, that team was. My owner was a grand man, such a man as I would like someday to be myself but can't quite cut it.

I had managed to slip the team out of town and presently there I was, in the country, before a farmhouse, the house in which that girl lived. I hollered to her. She came out to my call but her father came, too. He said she couldn't go.

The whole world was white that night. There must have been something white and swift and nice in me, in the team and in the girl. There were warm robes in the sleigh.

So the girl stood in tears on the porch of the house. Growling, her father went inside. I said nothing and the girl said nothing.

Suddenly she made a little run down to me and climbed into the sleigh. Her face was white like the night. "Quick," she said, and we drove off.

That was a ride. Once the black team ran away. We were crossing a bridge. The sound of their own hoofs on the floor of the bridge frightened the team. I let them run until they were tired of it but did manage to keep them in the road and the sleigh right side up.

And so my country girl and I rode in the white night like a prince and a princess—in the grand manner. What the father said to her when I took her home I don't know. You may be sure I avoided him. I got one cold, quick kiss in the darkness before the house and lit out.

And the man who owned the fine horses never knew. It was a lucky night for me.

"This wary winter that was white so long."

Wanting my youth back, of course. Walking in the white night in that field that Sunday night, every little bush and weed stood up straight and white. The sky was bluish-black overhead.

Thinking of youth, wanting my own youth to go on and on a long, long time, I began thinking how our town might be more gay.

It was then I wanted to be rich. "If I were only rich," I cried. Plans began to form in my mind. I would buy me a huge old house with a garden here in Marion.

The house would have huge rooms all with big open fires for cold nights and there would be a swimming pool in the garden back of the house.

I would publish my two Marion papers in rooms at the front of the house.

And I would have a library with many books and a place to dance and the Marion band would come and play for the dances on a Saturday night.

And there would be quiet nooks in the house and in the garden for old people to sit and for lovers.

And it would all be free.

And country people would come into town for the fun, and city people would come here to see us. I could think of many people I would like to have come.

Now and then perhaps a poet or a singer or a painter to spend a few days.

And I would walk around like a lord and edit my papers and dance with the pretty girls and wear the loudest clothes I could buy and stay young forever.

If I were only rich now.

All of this in my head as I walked in that field and in the white road and no one abroad but myself and saying over and over to myself words of that poet:

"This wary winter that was white so long."

THE BLACK HOLE OF MARION

April 12

This town of Marion, situated as it is in the very heart of one of the most lovely stretches of country this correspondent has ever seen, a fair town in a fair valley with softly rounded hills about it and full of good people, has in it a black hole that makes the nervous shudder to contemplate.

I refer to our county jail. It is a veritable pest hole. Go into it some day. Look about you. See what the prisoners in our jail are up against.

Well, you may answer, it is a place for criminals.

Not quite that. I myself was raised in a poor family. It was a family of boys. At a tender age we had to get out and scratch gravel. One of my younger brothers (he is dead now) went eastward from our middle-western country town, seeking work in one of the factories of the East. He had little money when he set out and had to beat his way on freight trains. Many a mile have I myself traveled in that way.

The point is that in a New York town he was arrested for vagrancy and kept in just such a pest hole as is maintained by Smyth County, and he was kept there for over two weeks.

He didn't want to send home for money because there was no money to spare at home.

Once, at Marion, Ohio, I was myself arrested as a suspect in connection with a diamond robbery. I had never heard of the robbery until the moment I was arrested. Some of our county officials may wonder why my sympathies are always with the man in trouble. The men at Marion sat and shouted at me, "You lie and you know you lie." I got out of that because, at that time, I had risen a bit in the world and had some friends.

To return to our county jail. Do not blame our county officials for the hole. There are two rooms downstairs and one up. Mr. and Mrs. Hopkins are doing mighty well with what they have to work with. The prisoners like and trust them. Our jailer and his wife are both kindly human beings.

There are two rooms downstairs and one up. One of the downstairs rooms is for women prisoners. It has two little cubby-hole windows and an open toilet, right in the open room. The women prisoners must sleep, eat and make all of their toilet arrangements in the one open room. Hardened women prisoners, syphilitics, tuberculars, dopes, etc., must go right in with the rest. Very often young girls are confined in the place.

Remember that not all the prisoners thrown into jail in a county-seat town are guilty. Many are merely suspect. They are cleared when they come to trial.

Of course, they are let out on bail if a responsible bondsman can be found, but suppose you are poor and unknown.

And now let us go into the men and boys' department. The law provides that these prisoners are to be kept in cages. The cages are some eighteen feet long by fifteen feet wide. In one of these cages at the present time there are eleven men. Some of them have been in there, they tell me, for months—twelve months, one of them. There is one open toilet in the cage and no bathing facilities. The boys tell me that at this time there is a syphilitic in there. They must use all of the facilities for bare, brutal living he uses. A tubercular case may be thrown in at any time. If there is no one to offer bail, guilty or innocent, he must stay until his case can be brought up in court. You know about the delay of courts. Suppose the delay went on while you waited in there.

Day after day, no place to exercise; diseased men, criminals, etc., in there with you. Eleven of you in a little cage eighteen feet long. Step it off on your parlor floor. Eleven of you in there jammed together, mind you.

In a cage upstairs the same condition. The state delaying about coming and getting men already committed to the penitentiary.

A few boys and men, in for minor offenses, wandering about the narrow room outside. Boys are put in there from the age of twelve years up.

It would sear your soul if you went to see it.

O, of course, it would raise taxes a bit if the county built a decent jail with decent toilet arrangements, a place to isolate diseased cases, a bit of a yard for exercise and a peep at the sun.

They have such places in penitentiaries, where men convicted of crime go.

And don't be so sure you or your boy won't get in there. A prominent young man was thrown in this receptacle for being drunk and disorderly. It can happen to anyone anytime.

The county that permits such conditions to go on is as guilty as the men who commit the crimes and are thrown in there for committing them.

A TOWN EYESORE

April 26

Since we have been editing the two Marion papers and all the time getting better and better acquainted with our fair town, we have been hoping that something would be done with what we have from time to time jokingly called "Mencken Park."

It is the prize eyesore of the town. Standing as it does just back of the courthouse, with a green, pleasant lawn in front, this lot is at present occupied by a building that would make a poor excuse for a cowshed.

The building itself is used to house the town machinery. In the yard beside it are piles of sand and crushed stone, iron pipe, empty tar barrels, and other junk of that sort. Since we have been here we must say that Mr. W. H. Wheeler and his helpers have been very nice about keeping the place as orderly as is possible.

It cannot be made a very pleasant place while it is used for its present purpose.

And it has seemed to us that another place, not so conspicuous, might well be found for this stuff.

Having something of the sort in mind, this editor recently made a proposal, in a conversation with some of his friends. He proposed that, if the town council would find some other place for the stuff now kept in this conspicuous place, he, or this paper, would spend some money to try and make this little plot of ground more pleasant and agreeable to the town.

Already some of our citizens are having pleasant hours in the park pitching horse shoes. It was the notion of this editor that if the town would clear this space and give permission, this editor would level off this little park, put green benches about it, and perhaps a strip of lawn around it and some shade trees.

If the papers cannot pay for it, then I'll write a story for some magazine and pay for it that way. It would be a more worthy cause than most of the story writers are up to most of the time.

It is our understanding that Mr. Charles Funk put this idea up to the Kiwanis Club but there was some misunderstanding. They seemed to think we were talking about a children's playground and the town, it seems, already has one.

We were thinking about a pleasant place here in the very heart of town, instead of an eyesore. The present place is in full sight from Main Street. It gives a bad impression of the town. Incidentally, a good many visitors come to this office—about everyone in the county at some time during the year. A lot of outside people come here, too.

If the town wants to take us up on this, we are ready to put up for our part of the job. What do you say, town council?

NOTE—It is our notion that when Mr. Funk and others put this matter up to the Kiwanis Club they talked about children's playgrounds, etc., etc., because—well, who wants to admit that what we want is a place where most of the children who do the playing are over—say, forty? It's pretty hard to own up to that sort of thing when you happen to be one of the children yourself.

A SUNDAY AFTERNOON

April 26

To walk with a man of Marion. Two grown men throwing stones at a bottle floating in the river.

The day raw. Going out on such a spring day like going into someone's bedroom in the early morning.

The year is all ready to put on its coat of green but is undressed yet.

How altogether different the lives of two men. O, man who has been in many places, cities, countries! There are two boys, also throwing stones. The man with me suddenly begins talking. He is telling about boys in a country schoolhouse, long ago, at the time of the Russian-Japanese War. There was a small stream beside the schoolhouse. They made boats of bits of wood, called them battleships. Then they floated them in the stream and pelted them with stones.

It was a day to make you recall other days. Winter has gone now but spring is not here. A few trees have blossomed. They will be frosted, being out so early.

People dressed in their Sunday best walking about. Tiny leaves, like squirrels' ears, on some of the trees. I am thinking about another spring day.

I am a young man again. With another young man I have been carousing in a French city. We have left the city in a cab at four in the morning, taking with us two women. Who are the women? We have picked them up in some café.

They were two American women. I remember one from Des Moines, Iowa. What were they? We piled them into a cab and drove off to an old medieval French town on a hill.

An old walled town. We found a café open and sat outdoors,

huddled in our overcoats. Our breakfast was served out there, seeing the sun come up.

A sudden quiet over all of us.

As my own mind is reaching back to that morning as I walk today, so on that morning all of our minds must have been reaching back to medieval days.

What happened on that day I can't remember. What became of the women I can't remember. No doubt, we presently returned to the city and parted.

I am walking in Marion with a Marion man. He is thinking of his boyhood. We talk of things far from our thought. We come to a bridge and cross it.

Thoughts drifting in people's minds. All the people talking of something outside their thoughts.

Men and women always meeting and parting like broken fragments of clouds in a vast sky.

BRAINS AND MORALS

April 26

The whole object of education is, or should be, to develop mind. The mind should be a thing that works. It should be able to pass judgment on events as they arise, make decisions.

There have been few enough good minds in the history of the world.

People have mind confused with learning. There have been more learned fools than wise ones.

Many people develop one sort of brain. For example, the man who can make money and is a fool in other things is not quite a fool. He isn't a fool about money.

And that is important. The trouble is that a one-sided man makes it too important. He judges everything by a money standard and gets everything crooked.

And morals also are largely a matter of brains. We are all driven through life by lusts. Why deny it? There is sex lust, food lust, lust for luxuries, for power.

The man with good brains simply recognizes his lusts as a part of his life and tries to handle them.

If he is an artist he tries to divert the energy arising from his lusts into channels of beauty. If he has any brains he knows what he is doing. Every artist worth his salt has always been full of lusts. Pretty little poets, lady authors, etc., may have no lusts but they remain "pretty."

Your son goes and gets drunk. He raises the very devil, perhaps smashes his automobile, and is lucky if he escapes killing someone. You crowd repentance on him. Try to make him think he has disgraced you forever. Well, why did he do it?

To be sure, he was driven on by some kind of excess energy within himself, and the chances are he did not have brains enough to direct his energy. Life grew dull to him. He was bored, wanted excitement. The trouble with most of your moral preachments is that you become a bore when you are getting them off.

And you are insincere, too. Your own lusts may just take another form. You eat, not like a man but like an animal.

Or you have a lust for money or power. To get it you will do anything. You see plenty of such men—in politics, for example.

Men who will lie, cheat, steal, sell out their friend politically, and who in other walks of life are fair enough men.

Well, that is just a form of lust, too. It is political drunkenness. There are various kinds of drunkenness in this world.

The man of brains has found out that he has to adjust himself to life and, most of all, to himself. Take the matter of drink. I should think the man of sense would see it as not a moral question at all.

It is a matter of good sense. If a man cannot drink without making a fool of himself and hurting others he should let drink alone.

He should let alone anything he can't handle.

Few men ever get far enough with the development of mind to quite realize there is one thing they have to stay with always, as long as they live—that is themselves.

A man may move to a new town, get a new wife, a new house, a new suit of clothes. He is still himself.

I have myself learned to look at my body as a house in which I must live until I die. I want it to be a fairly clean, comfortable house. I do not like making a muss in the house. I have to sleep there. My thoughts dwell there.

If I let my body get too gross, if I gobble too much food, drink too much, get too fat, my house is an uncomfortable place in which to live.

I do not like it nor do I like myself.

To be sure, there is a challenge in all this. Keep your house as clean as you can. Wash the windows and the doorsills. You cannot live well in a filthy place.

And do not be sick. The sick man is more than half a rascal. He may only be sick because he hasn't the courage to clean house. Many sick people are bullies—they use sickness as a club to beat others.

The house is a body in which the mind, the spirit, and the imagination must dwell until we die. A little decent paganism wouldn't hurt most of us. We ought to try to be a bit less mixed about morals and a bit more clear about mind.

A little more decent faith in the house in which we live—the house that is the body—less thinking about death and more about living, more self-respect.

If that be paganism, make the most of it.

THE ANSWER

June 14

Dear Henry Goodman:*

After all—you must admit—it is a fairly large-sized order you have given here. I really cannot attempt to do it. I do not like such pawing over of my past emotions. Sometimes it is inevitable. I have put a character in a book. There is the book of mine called *A Story Teller's Story*. That isn't autobiography. It is really a novel—of the mind of a man, let us say, of a man who happened to be a writer.

You are bound to find that most of your students will be thinking of writing as a way to make a living, to attain success, attract attention to themselves. The formulas are infinitely better for them. If they follow the formulas they will be much more likely to succeed.

Of course, all kinds of emotions are stirring about in them. So are they in my colored cook, in the first man I meet when I go out into the street. And I understand your feelings, too. You do not like the cheap little channels into which human emotions are poured in the ordinary, conventional short story in the magazines.

You would like all of these young writers to be artists. Well, I would like all people to be lovers but do not know how to bring it about. I suppose there are only two sorts of really nice people in the world, the lover in love or the artist at work.

You wouldn't attempt to give a course in love-making, would you, or get out a book of explanations by well-known lovers?

How am I to attempt to lay down a formula for the channeling of the emotions of these young people?

Let us say I am in love. God knows, I have been many times. I see or meet some woman who is beautiful to me. I want her. How

* Henry Goodman, a teacher at Hunter College, had asked Anderson to state his feelings about the creative process.

am I to get her? Well, I send her flowers and candy. I go to see her. Alas, this is a test for me. Am I up to it? Many doubts assail me. I walk with her under trees. It may be that I manage to get her off somewhere where we can be alone together. This would be difficult where I am now living, in a small town. In a city it might be managed better. But I am getting older now. It may be I am more discriminating. I do not fall in love so often or write so many stories.

But be that as it may, let us say I have pulled this matter off. I have got my lady to the seashore and am walking with her. On a certain afternoon, when I am with her, the matter between us is decided.

I come home from there, my dear man, and you take me aside. "I want you to tell my students just how it was done. What did you say to her? Repeat your words. Perhaps it was something in your eyes. Make your eyes look as they did at that moment. My students are worthy young men and women. They want to succeed in love. At the critical moment did you feel a certain emotion? Please feel it again now. My students want to see how you look when you feel it."

You see the probabilities are that [Manuel] Komroff, [Waldo] Frank, and Miss Zona Gale were talking nonsense. When they really do it they cannot tell how they do it. Their explanations are as likely to be wrong as right.

You know, that is one thing I like about painters. Most of them let someone else do the explaining. They paint. Ask one of them to tell you how he felt at a certain moment, how he held the brush in his hand, etc., etc., and he would tell you to go to Pittsburgh.

And he would do it for just the reasons suggested above.

For each man and woman his own reactions to life, and life happens to be the writer's materials. If you are to have any individuality as a workman, you have to go alone through the struggle to find expression for what you feel. You have, of course, to train your hand and your eye. Just because you ache to do something is no sign you can do it. Talent is given you. You have it or you haven't. A real writer shows himself a writer in every sentence he writes.

The training is another matter. It is a question of how keen is the desire, how much patience and perseverance there is. Sometimes I think it largely a matter of physical strength. How much disappointment can you stand before you throw up the sponge.

Right now, at this moment, I have a hundred stories in me I am not man enough to write as they should be written. How am I to tell another man how to do what I cannot myself do?

A DECLARATION

June 21

This editor is so devoted to his task of editing that he lives in one of the apartments above the printshop. There are three of these apartments. Mayor Dickinson lives in one and Preston Collins in another. They are both peaceful men and good neighbors, but Mr. Dickinson is mayor. We are very thankful that he did not run for re-election and that Dr. Brown, who was elected, does not live in our neighborhood.

You are going to have a sweet time as mayor, Doc. Well, you will go to sleep. You will be dreaming blithely of your political policy—that is to say, "More and Better," whatever that means—and someone will go out and commit a felony or a misdemeanor or an immorality of some sort.

Then the felon will arrive under your window in a large car. Officers will be in charge. Everyone will begin calling in loud voices. "O, Doc," they will call. Well, they want to be bailed out or something. They will wake you up and wake up the whole neighborhood. Everyone will lie awake wondering who they are and what they did.

I suggest this, Doc. Have a grandstand put up before your house. I am not sure where you live but think it must be up on hospital hill. I hope it is. Most of the town council are from up there.

Well, you have the grandstand built and, after these noisy felons have gone away, you go out in your pajamas—no need dressing—and stand on the grandstand and in a loud voice tell the neighbors who they were and what they did.

Then their curiosity will be still and they can sleep. You will be a good neighbor. If you are foolish enough to want to be re-elected, it will be a cinch.

HOT TIMES IN SUGAR GROVE

July 5

It was a gorgeous Sunday. The editor was driving over the mountains. At Sugar Grove he saw the sheriff, Mr. Dillard, and Hi Whistman. "Something doing here," says the editor to himself and was glad they did not know all he knew about his past.

Elsewhere in this paper you will see where the sheriff and Hi got two over at Sugar Grove on Saturday. On Sunday they got three more—W. T. Ashland, Bert Ashland, and Cox Bullings. They were taken before Squire Schuller and each fined $15.75. Bert and W. T. Ashland paid up and were let go. Cox Bullings, he says, didn't have the price. They brought him to town and lodged him in jail.

A fine moonlight night. No night to be in jail. No night to be drunk either. The editor got drunk on moonlight coming home over the beautiful Slemp Mountain road Sunday night, but if the sheriff and Hi had searched him they wouldn't have found a thing. Come on, you searchers. Search the sky and the stars and the low gray clouds that lie over the mountains.

All the prohibition in the world can't stop the editor getting on his own kind of a jag on a night like Sunday night.

But back to Sugar Grove. Teas, it seems, was feeling all swelled up with virtue because Sugar Grove had been so wicked. Five in two days. So up goes Dillard and Hi and find a 60-gallon still in the old vacant Barton house near Teas. Pride goeth before a fall. And a prohibition meeting going on in Marion, too. I hope they don't prohibit the editor's kind of a jag. We have them there. They can't take the stars out of the sky or change the lovely evening shapes of our hills.

THE NEWSPAPER OFFICE

July 12

Spent an evening in the office of a city newspaper. Everything was standing waiting. The paper was to go to press at two o'clock to catch out-going trains. At Houston the Democratic Convention was going on. It was understood that Mr. Smith would get the nomination, but the big question in this newspaper office was this: will they get at it in time to catch our out-going trains?

A slight nervousness, everything a bit tense. Again, I was glad that my own newspaper experience was confined to our own little weeklies.

No one expects us to be down to the minute. What we have got to do is to make a readable paper—gather the home news.

What pleases me most in the big newspaper offices is the composing room and the press room. Any man who has seen the big modern presses turn out daily papers will never forget the experience. If I were a city newspaperman I would insist on working down in the press room. I would set up a little desk there and do my writing there, in the presence of the presses.

I suggested this idea once to a New York newspaperman, but he said it was not practical. To me it seemed that, if men had to work in the presence of the great presses, presently there would be a new dignity creep into their work. Suppose a man could write prose as fine as these presses. Or something worthy of the linotype machine.

Suppose a man could write prose that did its work as smoothly and well as a modern automobile.

In spite of all their efforts to prevent it, the modern newspaper, like most modern things, has lost all track of life. Life has pretty nearly been syndicated out of it.

In almost every factory the men look small beside the machines they operate. It is true in the newspaper office surely.

What a place is the modern newspaper composing room. There are the long batteries of machines, linotypes, so marvelously accurate. Then the whole process of preparing and locking the forme. The new machine that casts individual lines of type of any size for the advertising pages.

Then the rooms where the mats are made and the formes cast for the big presses.

I remember once standing in the press room of a New York newspaper. The editor-in-chief was there. The afternoon paper was just going to press.

The great rolls of paper were swung into place. The huge presses were threaded as a woman might thread a needle. We stood watching. The presses began to run.

Faster, faster, faster. The papers were dropping from the presses like snowflakes in a storm. The man picked one up and handed it to me. We stood looking at each other and at the presses. The same thought was in both our minds. "We are in the same position all modern men are in," he said. "The machine has got far ahead of man. We cannot catch up to it."

He meant clearly that there was nothing in the paper being printed in the great presses with anything like the dignity and worth of the presses themselves.

EDITORIAL STATEMENT

July 19

The *Marion Democrat* and the *Smyth County News* are, respectively, a Democratic and a Republican paper. The editor is not stating his own position in this fight. He owns and edits the papers.

Our purpose is to run newspapers. Political matter is not going to swamp news in either of our papers. Already we have on our hooks enough political matter to pretty near fill both papers, each issue for weeks.

We are going to put in what we can. It will appear on our editorial page.

If you have something—being a Republican—that you think will slay Al Smith, or that—being a Democrat—will make Mr. Hoover ashamed he is alive, and can't get it in the papers this week or next, don't blame us.

We don't mind war—go to it.

But we are running newspapers first, last, and all the time.

And we will be running them when this fight is over.

IN COON HOLLOW

July 26

The boss says, "You write a real piece about Coon Hollow." He says, "I want to see if you can write." Says I, "Do you mean taking the bars down?" I says, "Do you mean telling some of the things that do happen?" "Shoot," says he.

This happened last week. Mrs.—well, I won't put her name. I'll call her Mrs. Smith. I'll give her a made-up name, same as the boss does when he throws his yarns.

But this isn't any yarn. This is the cold, gray, early-morning truth. Mrs. Smith, up toward Johnson's Cove, had a pretty good man. They bought thirty acres of land. Mrs. Smith had six kids by her man before she got to cutting up.

They didn't have their farm paid for. I guess they had too many kids.

So Smith he went out to West Virginia to work in the coal fields out there. His oldest boy, Hy Smith, he went, too.

So, Mrs. Smith, I guess she was kind of discouraged and a kind of hard-bitten woman she was, too, and so she goes to getting gay with other men. As poor as we are, we mountain people, we are like men everywhere, I guess. Give us a loose woman around and we'll go to her, I guess.

And so a lot of men did. Mrs. Smith's husband died over in the coal mines—got killed over there.

And so Mrs. Smith kept cutting her didoes and young Hy Smith, her oldest son, was working over there in the coal mines and sending his wages to pay for the place. He got the place paid for, too.

And while he was doing it his maw had two more kids.

So she and the men that had got to coming to see her kept raising hallelujah up there in the Cove. So Hy comes home one day last week and has his mother arrested for being what she is. Mayor Dickinson comes over to hear the case and Andy Funk comes. Two fellows from up the Cove gets up and swears. "Were you up there?" "Yes." "Did you pay money?" "No," they says, "we hoed corn."

So Mayor Dickinson says to Hy, "What about these kids?" Hy says, "I'll take care of all of the kids that belonged to my paw, that got killed in the mines." He says, "Let the corn-hoers take care of the rest."

So they takes Mrs. Smith to jail in Marion and she has one of the corn-hoers' kids with her. So there now and that's one.

So here's another. There is a girl named Lizzy up around the Cove country but not living in it. She is only thirteen or maybe fourteen years old. What she is going to turn out to be I don't know. She's a pretty girl. Life is pretty raw in some of these farms.

She was walking in the road. This will be a week ago last Saturday. Some fellows come along and they had a Ford. They had some liquor in it, too. They says to Lizzy, "Do you want to go along with us?" "Yes," Lizzy says. She was bored stiff, I guess, like I get sometimes.

So they takes Lizzy along with them and they go over to Scratch Gravel, near Marion. They stays at a house over there. Well, they all got drunk. They raised hallelujah over there, too.

Someone phoned the sheriff in Marion and he comes out. When the fellows see him coming they all lit out. "Who were they?" the sheriff asks but Lizzy won't tell. I guess she figured if she was in dutch it was her own fault.

There was nothing to do with Lizzy and so they let her come on home. She lied, of course, when she got home. She had to square herself if she could. She said they abducted her. "Who was it?" says her paw and her brother. I guess if he knew who it was it would be pretty near a shooting matter with him. But she won't tell.

So there you are. That's the kind of thing that happens sometimes. The boss wanted me to tear the lid off once, tell some of the things that really do happen back in these mountains. So I said I'd do it and see whether or not he would print it. If he does I'm sure I won't care. BUCK FEVER.

CONTENTED TAR BARRELS

August 9

The boss is always giving me fool assignments. The other day he wanted me to go on down to the new home of the town machinery and tar barrels and see how they were getting along in their new home. Doc Brown and Bill Todd went down with me.

It is sure fine down there. I never saw tar barrels looking better in my life. Their new home is in a nice big old Southern antique house, the grounds of which are washed by Staley's Creek. We all had a nice time down there. Mr. Wheeler, assisted by Bill Grundy, poured tea.

Then we stood around a while. "I expect your boss will want you to write this up in some fool way, eh?" said Doc Brown. "Don't you like to be in the paper, Doc?" I said. "No," said Doc. "Then for why did you run for mayor?" I said. I had him there.

We asked Bill Todd how he liked the tar barrels in the new place. "Fine," Bill said. Bill has an affectionate nature. He went over and patted one of the tar barrels on the shoulder. It was the first time that particular tar barrel had ever had that kind of individual attention from a town official. It almost fell off the pile.

Well, we looked around at the sand scrapers and the nice pile of sand and the road rollers and all. It was as nice a walk as ever we took. Everything down there is dry, roomy, and out of the way. Mr. Wheeler and his boys have done a good job. They have got a swell blacksmith shop and everything they need. BUCK FEVER.

IN THE DEWY MORN

August 9

The birds flying over Overbay Hollow. This isn't Coon Hollow. This is up by Atkins.

Anyway, George Gullion and Sam Seabolt went up there in the dewy morn, on Thursday of last week. They got a still out of there. It was full of mash. Not a soul around. George said it was fine to hear the little birds sing.

But if you want to take the pledge you should have seen the barrel they were making it in. Emmett Thomas says they keep stealing his oil barrels, too. This one was as black and dirty an old piece of furniture as you ever saw. The prohibitionists may or may not be drying up the American people, but they are sure managing it so they have to drink some horrible stuff. One look at that still and, if you have any taste left, you'd quit for good.

THEY SURE DO

August 16

"Why," says a well-known citizen of Marion, "if there is any drinking nowadays I don't see it." That same day the editor drove to his farm. At one spot there was a Ford parked across the road with three drunken men in it asleep. The editor finally awoke them. They managed to push the car off the road, falling down several times in doing it. They even mis-called us "Buck." But Buck is a young and handsome man. "Why, hello, Buck," they said. The editor went on to his farm and came back to Marion. Someone told him that Herbert Fry, of Saltville, had been caught, red-handed, at a still by officers Holmes and Thompson and was in town trying to get bail. Hy Whistman had just arrested Reves Rolland. Reves, it seems, was full of corn and thought he was a wild and woolly man. He drove around shouting and waving a gun. He got down to Luther Buchanan's store, on South Fork, and, it is said, rode around the store shooting in.

Sheriff Dillard had just been out in the South Fork neighborhood and had got one of the Dipes boys. He was accused both of being drunk and of selling.

Si Price, over at Chilhowie, gathered up Russ Hankley. Russ had bought some alcorub to rub on. It smelled too good, he said; so he drank it. It seemed to get results.

Si was also chasing Charlie Hicks of Charlotts Creek, which is at the entrance of Cleghorn Valley. Charley got filled up and wanted to fight someone. There was no one else about; so he fought his sister.

It is said the sister whipped him. Well, it seems they do it.

O! MARION

August 23

Sweet town in the hills. Some of the summer days are hot, but cool breezes come down from the hills in the evening. On court days the country people are out in droves. Tall mountain men come with their tall wives and their armies of children. There is no race suicide in these hills.

And there are the people from the fat valleys, where the great steers stand belly-deep in the grass. They come in big cars with their daughters and sons, home from college.

On Saturday afternoons the streets are lined with cars. There are pretty girls here. Buck Fever and other young fellows are walking down "The Rialto" looking at them.

On the Rialto also and over on the courthouse steps are older men. They are discussing the affairs of the state. Moral laws are being laid down. They may be looking at the handsome girls and women, too, but they pretend not to be. On cold days they will move inside the courthouse. In the clerk's and treasurer's office they will keep right on solving the same problems.

Few towns on this old earth are as happily situated as our sweet town of Marion. Hills and wooded heights climb up in all directions. Although the town is small there are two hotels here that you would have to go to a big city to find the like of. There is good cooking, too. Good cooking and good eating are a tradition in this section of Southwest Virginia, both for animals and men.

It is a country of pure-bred cattle, sheep, hogs, and dogs. Great orchards blossom here in the spring and hang heavy with apples in the fall.

In the hills there are pheasants and birds and in the fall men come and go through the streets with full game bags. There are some fine shots here.

Fishing, too—bass in the rivers and trout in the mountain streams. Within two hours' drive of Marion, over lovely hill roads, are at least a half dozen rivers and perhaps twenty or thirty mountain creeks.

It is a country for the city man to visit. Artists who have been here have been deeply stirred by the shapes of our hills and the riots of colors in the fall.

Hunters and fishermen might come here, too. It isn't a place to slaughter fish or game. You have to work for your bag here but it is here to get.

There is an odd illusion in many minds—at a distance from the mountains—about our mountain people. Often there is among them a fierce kind of loyalty and an equally fierce hatred. The notion that there is danger for an outsider going among them is one of the jokes of the world. Never a more hospitable people walked the earth. I have seen among them some of the handsomest men and women of America, and the gentlest.

The basic stock of this whole section is Old American. The quaint, early-English speech of the hills still lingers on the lips of the town people.

Marion is a town neither too good nor too bad. Men and women sin and pay the price of sin. There are trials in the courthouse. Blockaders, moonshiners are caught and pay the price of being caught. We have our liars and our honest men. It is an intensely human place, be sure of that. . . .

THE FAIR

August 23

The fair is an institution as old as mankind. When Caesar went up into the wilds of Germany he found towns and villages there in the forests. Annual fairs were held there among the wild men in the German forests as they are held in American towns today. Well, there were the broad-shouldered wild men of the forests riding their wild horses. There were exhibits, too. The horse traders were there.

The same thing going on in far China and Tibet. Marco Polo, the first great traveler, speaks of the fairs of the Far East.

And on the Russian steppes and in cold Siberia other fairs being held.

Normal men have always loved horses. The automobile has rather taken the horse out of every-day life. For a time it was thought the horse might disappear out of our civilization.

Indications are, however, that the horse is here to stay. Horseracing is regaining all of its old popularity. Vast crowds in the cities now go to see the runners, the trotters, and pacers. Purses are higher than ever. The horse has become an aristocrat.

O, the horse, the horse. This writer remembers when he was a young boy. He went horse crazy once. Well, he got a job with a string of trotters and pacers. It was a lowly job. He was a groom and went about in horsey, evil-smelling pants. Well does he remember when he came home and told his mother what he was going to do. There were tears in her eyes. She thought the association of the tracks would be bad for her son.

Still she was one who hated to cross a son of hers. "If it gives you satisfaction, go ahead." The son did go ahead.

I dare say the associations were bad, too. What profanity the boy heard! There were men about the stables who were artists at it.

Tough women hanging about, too—and con men, flash men of all sorts.

The boy made friendships there he will never forget. There was Bert, that big Negro with the big fists and the laugh; Long John Bottsford, a fellow groom; Billy Stark, the driver. Once he found a man who was with a little fake show. You paid ten cents and got a picture of your future sweetheart. The show had trouble sometimes; something slipped. One country white girl got a picture of a gigantic Negro and another country girl a picture of a bulldog. That one gave the showman a black eye.

The fellow who ran that show walking about in strange towns with the editor talking, I remember, of poetry. We talked of Shelley. Would you believe that? He could quote whole poems.

And there was a fellow who was the wild man in a pit show. He claimed to have been a Virginia gentleman and a landowner once. Drink, he said, had brought him down. After the crowds had gone in the evening, he used to sit with us and lie and lie about his past.

It was good lying. We learned a lot from that one.

And the horses and the cattle and the bands and the shows and the crowds.

And the glorious day when the boss got sick and let us drive Solarian, that great pacer, in the last heat of the free-for-all pace. And we won it, too, not through any merit of our own but because Solarian only needed a light boy up who could hold the reins and talk to him to win it himself.

And then our name in the paper, to be mailed home proudly to Mother. And after the fairs were over in the fall going home, ourselves to brag and brag and tell some of our own lies.

Lives there a man with soul so dead who never to himself has said: "What ho for the fair!" Come on, let's all go.

MAMIE GOT CAUGHT

August 23

Well, well, here we are. Smyth County is getting more and more like Manhattan and Cook County, Illinois. Now we can have a bootleg queen. Can you beat that? Talk about being in style!

Our bootleg queen is Mamie Palmer. No, she doesn't live here. She was caught here. But we do not see why we should not claim Mamie, just the same. What ho, for the modern world.

Mamie has been running the stuff for several years, although she is only twenty-six. She is a neat-looking little woman, too. Her home, she says, is at Northfork, West Virginia.

Mamie has for years been running liquor out of the mountains south of Marion and on into the North. She has owned several large cars and, we gather, has done well. Once, she says, she got into a tight hole while driving a big Buick. They were hot on her trail. This was in Kentucky. That time she drove her car into a river and lit out.

This time Sheriff Dillard and officer Thompson of Saltville just stopped her on the highway. They had seen her making regular trips through the county and had got suspicious. A search of the car revealed a fairly good-sized load. She is in jail in Marion now. What ho, for the modern world.*

* This and two subsequent stories (September 13 and October 25, 1928) supplied the plot for Anderson's last novel, *Kit Brandon* (New York: Charles Scribner's Sons, 1936).

SOLILOQUY

August 30

I am constantly wondering about other men, how they manage to live. Well, there they are and there am I. Sometimes the whole idea of everyday life seems to me distorted, a little crazy.

I am thinking constantly of what I myself should be. Well, what I would like to be.

I would like to be a man of more dignity. I would like not to hurt anyone.

There are so few nights when I can go to bed with any satisfaction to myself. At night I go into my own room and sit down. I read perhaps a newspaper. The newspaper is an odd thing, too. There is the world spread out before me—pride, crime, ambition. How many pitiful things happen.

Today I got a letter from an old friend. He was a man of forty-two and fell in love with a young girl. How beautiful she seemed to him. He let his whole life be wrapped up in her. Once, a year or two ago, when I saw him last, he talked to me about it.

"It is dangerous," he said, "to be so absorbed in another but what am I to do? I cannot bear the idea of trying to think of myself, live for myself."

He thought I was a luckier man than he was. He spoke of that. "You are not as dependent on people as I am," he said. He had the notion that my writing answered all the needs of my own nature. "It is something into which you can throw yourself," he said.

Well, sometimes—rarely—I can. Mostly, I cannot.

Now my friend's wife has left him. She has fallen in love with a man nearer her own age. She came and told him about it. He made no fuss. "All right," he said to her, "I will do what I can." He has gone away from the city in which he has been living with her. In the meantime he provides her with money with which to live.

Presently she will get a divorce. She will, I fancy, marry the other man.

And there is my friend sitting bitterly in his room writing to me. That is one of the sort of things that happen in this world. He is trying to be philosophic about it, to laugh.

His letter is a long one. He is trying to take it all as a part of life. "You bet and sometimes you lose," he says.

My mail is filled with all sorts of things. I am a man to whom people write letters. It is because of my books. I have written some story that has touched closely some man or woman. They feel close to me. A long letter sometimes results.

There is a woman in the East somewhere. She has centered her whole life about a little dog. The dog and the woman were on a beach. The moonlight was streaming down.

The little dog began to play. He ran madly in the moonlight. There may have been a kind of madness in the woman, too. She had been ill for a long time. For some reason, when she went home, she sat down and wrote me a long letter. She described the moonlight, the sea, the dark look of the land behind her.

Her writing to me to describe all this, of course, meant nothing. In a certain story of mine, I once described some dogs, gone mad with moonlight.* She remembered that and so, after she had come in from her walk, she wrote to me.

She took my name out of the front of the book and wrote me in care of my publishers.

She told me a story, too, that in an odd way capped the story told in the letter of my man friend.

She had been loved, in early life, by a man of whom she grew tired. She left him for another man. This happens pretty often in modern life.

Later she regretted what she had done. The second man grew tired of her, she said. He left her and she was alone. She lives alone. She has enough money to live comfortably.

I am in my room late at night and I sit there thinking. Sometimes I lie awake for hours after I go to bed. My room faces the town jail.

* "Death in the Woods," *American Mercury*, IX (September, 1926), 7–13; title story for Anderson's last collection of stories (New York: Liveright, Inc., 1933).

I think of the men and women in jail. I think of friends kept and friends lost. I have lost a good many friends through my own foolishness.

This writing is a dangerous business, too. Every writer has a desire to be clever. But cleverness is very dangerous. In being clever you sacrifice someone. You rob them of their dignity.

That ought never to be done. Every man or woman should be left their self-respect.

For example, in New York recently, I came face to face with a man who was my friend for a long time. He is a rather famous man, a writer. One day he sat writing. He thought up a very clever and rather nasty phrase about me. It was one of those phrases close to the truth and yet not true. Once I was broke and was lecturing before a large audience in Brooklyn. I was doing it to get some money with which to live. Some man in the audience suddenly got up and repeated that clever and rather nasty phrase. I was humiliated before a crowd of people.

I see people trying to humiliate each other all the time. It happens almost every time I hear men talking together on the streets here in my town. It happens everywhere.

I do it sometimes in my papers, too. I try not to do it but I do. The trouble with writing for a newspaper is that your stuff goes to press too soon. More than once I have awakened in the middle of the night. A day or two before, I had written something I thought was funny. Perhaps it was funny, too, but at someone else's expense. Sometimes I get up early and run downstairs into the print-shop to throw something of that sort out of the paper.

I am trying to give you here a picture of a man's thoughts, as he sits in his room at night or after he has gone to bed and is lying quietly there.

Sharp pangs of regret, a feeling of cheapness. Often I lie in bed thus for hours thinking these thoughts. I wonder how many others are doing the same thing. "I am a muddler in life," I say to myself. I wonder how many others are saying the same thing.

I think I must have become a writer because of this trick in myself. I could not bear thinking of myself when I was alone and so I tried valiantly to think of others.

I began with people I knew. I tried to be someone else.

I imagined myself being a horseman, racing horses on the race tracks. I tried to imagine myself rich, or poor, a youth, an old man, a United States senator, a sport, a woman, a young girl. I remembered little things I had heard people say.

There was a man walked in a certain way. Another man was always saying disagreeable things to people. There are all sorts of people everywhere. They are doing and saying all sorts of things. They are actuated by all sorts of desires and ambitions.

You cannot think far into other lives without becoming intensely humble. How do people manage as well as they do?

The habit of trying to be someone other than myself has grown on me. I do it constantly. I remember once being a murderer—in fancy, of course. I began having all of the thoughts of that man. There was a tense moment while the desire to kill was growing in my man's mind. It became a definite thing. He did kill. While he was killing his man I sat writing. This was on the deck of a steamer at sea. I remember how vivid everything was. I was thinking every thought the man thought, having his emotions. He got his man killed. I got through describing it all.

Just then a man came along and spoke to me. "Hello," he said. His voice startled me so that I came near leaping into the sea. The world I had been in, in which I had killed a man, was ten times more real than the real world. The man's voice had jerked me back too suddenly into the real world. I turned and walked rapidly away from him and went into my stateroom. I stood inside the room shivering, although it was a warm day. If I had not been a writer or a painter or some kind of an artist, I would have had to live too much with myself. I could not have stood it. Long ago I would have gone mad.

O GOODY

September 6

The nymphs are dancing in Sherwood Forest. See their little white legs. See them under the tall trees. They are scattering flowers. It is because Burt Dickinson is no longer mayor. Doc Brown is mayor now. He does not live down this way, at the edge of Sherwood Forest. He lives somewhere else.

Now when someone gets drunk and gets arrested at two o'clock in the morning, they will not come down here, at the edge of the forest, and stand in the road and shout. If county prosecutor Funk comes down here now and tries anything like that, awakening the gentle editor from his beauty sleep, he will get shot; hot water, boiling oil will be poured down on his gray head. He will be bitten by snakes. The tongue will cleave to the roof of his mouth.

Doc Brown, you may be a good mayor or you may not, but we greet you. We are happy. O, goody. Do the best you can, Doc. We will support you valiantly. We do not want Burt back in. We want him to be a quiet, peaceful citizen. We want him to practice law, preferably civil cases.

We have been asked by some of our subscribers to say what we think of the voices of some of our civic officials, calling to the mayor in the night. People who live up Doc Brown's way want to know.

Well, Funk has the worst voice, and the nicest one belongs to Si Price. Sheriff Dillard's voice has a rather nice note of freshness in it. It comes, we think, from being out so much at night.

And Mr. Hopkins' voice, and George Gullion's and Hy Whistman's, to say nothing of Mr. Thompson's of Saltville. That crowd should get up a quartette. They should sing at fairs. They should sing anywhere except at the edge of Sherwood Forest when the nymphs are trying to doze. Doc Brown's neighbors are going to like this crowd. There won't any of them need radios. O goody.

FALL

September 13

The change from summer to fall comes as suddenly and as subtly as the change in a child that becomes suddenly no longer a child.

Fall is here. The summer is gone. There is a new feeling in the sky, in trees, in the grass underfoot.

The summer went away like a bird that flies into a bush. There may be hot, sunshiny days yet but they will be fall days. With this writer it came after the rain that wiped out the last two days of our fair. They had but one horse race on Thursday. The trotters came out but the mud was too deep for them.

Some runners came out and ran, slashing through the mud. It was as though they were throwing summer out from their flying heels.

Then three days' solid rain. A cold clear day, a gray day, and then more rain. Summer was having a hard time getting away. The gray clouds were a cloak, concealing her departure.

She is gone now. It is fall. It can be a glorious time in this country but it is not summer.

Alas, this editor was born poor. Winter is ahead. As a child the coming of winter always brought fear of cold and hunger. The old dread holds. In contemplation of winter I am always afraid.

(photograph supplied by Walt Sanders, Black Star Publishing Company, Inc.)

Sherwood and Robert Lane Anderson in the Printshop at Marion, Virginia

"Henry Mencken Park," Marion's Machinery Dump Facing Marion Publishing Company

GOING TO NEBO

September 13

A man who takes our paper, a New York man, wrote to say that sometime before he dies he wants to go to Nebo.

We did not publish all of his letter. The man has never been in Smyth County. He was born in Europe and came here to America as a young man.

He happened to see our paper and liked it.

For one thing the names of people and places caught his fancy. Chatham Hill, Sugar Grove, Nebo.

There were accounts of the doings of the people. Now it is corn-planting time in the spring. The bees are coming out. The New York man, as he reads the paper, sees a little town in the mountains; he sees fields about the town.

He says someday he will go to Nebo. He does not mean that.

He merely means that he likes to have a town about which his fancy can play—an American town, far away somewhere, far away from city street, noise, the roar of life—about which he can dream.

In his daydreams, he says, Nebo is a happy land. There are no deaths there. Fair young women do not grow old and sicken and die.

There are no crop failures. There is nothing mean in the men.

It rains sometimes, just enough to make the crops grow luxuriously, but for the most part there is sunshine.

People singing as they walk in the roads or work in the field. In the Nebo of the New York man's daydreams, the women must all be fair and the men handsome.

And it is, of course, a land of love. Affection rules the lives of all the people.

No matter what a man of Nebo does, the others understand that his motive must have been all right.

The New York man says that, in his daydream Nebo, there are things that never happen. There are no lawsuits. Men and women who are married do not quarrel.

Well, for example, if a woman there falls in love with a man and another man loves her, the man who has lost out takes the loss as best he can.

It may be he goes into the woods and cries.

The New York man says that once, in his daydream, he saw such a man in a wood.

He went up and put his arms about the man's shoulder.

They walked together in the road. He tried to make the man understand his sympathy.

It was something lost, as things are lost—money lost, friends lost.

To lose a part of life. That, he says, is understood in Nebo.

He says everything is understood there because affection rules.

No one there is poor and no one sick.

The people love their hills and their fields. Because they love the fields they are careful with them. They would no more starve a field than a child.

The New York man says the name "Nebo" has got fixed in his fancy. He may never actually go there but in his daydreams he will go a thousand times.

"If," he says, "you see me in New York, someday, stopping to smile in the midst of a hurried, worried day, if you see my nerves relax, if I am suddenly absent-minded, you will know that, for the moment, I have fled away from my life here in New York and, as in my daydreams at least, I am on the road to Nebo."

MAMIE PALMER, BOOTLEG QUEEN, IN DYING CONDITION

September 13

Mamie Palmer, the young woman who was picked up with a load of booze by the sheriff some time ago, is in a bad condition. She went before the grand jury and plead guilty.

In the meantime it had been found that she was in an advanced state of tuberculosis.

Her condition has now become so bad that today Judge Stewart telegraphed Governor Byrd asking that she be pardoned. Lying in the jail in this condition, she is, of course, a menace to all the other prisoners. Even though we may feel that the guilty deserves to be compelled to take such chances—a very doubtful human point of view—how about the other prisoners, either not guilty or not proven guilty?

Our jail conditions here are terrible. Because the conditions in most county jails everywhere are bad is but little excuse. In Marion we have also a state hospital. Often men from the hospital, mental defectives, get out and get drunk. They are thrown in jail. Syphilitics and tuberculars are thrown in there. In these days of automobile accidents, bootleggers, etc., any man might be thrown in there. A disease might be contracted that would result in slow, horrible death.

The county jail and the Negro school building are the two Marion sore spots, both unsanitary, either one likely at any time to spread disease through the entire community.

THE MODERN AGE

September 13

The editor and his wife to see some pictures thrown on the screen at the office of Sprinkle Motors. It was night. The room was darkened. There was a young man there from the factory. The pictures were all concerned with tests made in the modern great automobile factory.

The exhibition made me determined to get some magazine to send me out to Detroit. I want to spend a day or two in one of these factories looking about. I would like to talk to the workmen there.

From these pictures, taken largely from the testing side of modern manufacture, most of the men employed are young men. The colleges must be turning out an endless number of these young scientists.

I was curious to see the faces of the workmen in the factories. The pictures were not large enough.

With me, always, the man is the most interesting side of any such industry. Who can doubt the efficiency of the cars made with such elaborate precaution against mistakes? Of course, they are all right. Everything used is tested to an extent almost unbelievable. It must be so in all the later great manufacturing organizations, and the larger the organization the more careful the tests of parts and materials can be. It is so because cost can be distributed over a greater number of cars.

Who can doubt that we could make each copy of this paper infinitely cheaper if we had a circulation of millions?

But there is always something lost. The something lost is of interest to me, too.

O, it is not in manufacture. The amount given for the money cannot be criticized. It makes no difference to me that a few men, controlling these great industries, get enormously rich.

I do not think it matters so much who gets very rich. Who wants to be very rich? To want it is childish and foolish.

When you pass a certain point in the accumulation of money, money also loses its significance. How many men in New York to whom it makes no difference whether the house in which they live costs them, per month to maintain, a thousand or fifty thousand?

There is a sense in which these men are truly royal. They are royal about things that concern you and me closely enough.

As the young salesman from the factory talked, I watched him closely, too. He was a nice young man. He was saying certain words. In how many places had he been saying the same words?

Significant words, too. He had in some way lost the significance of the words he said. Perhaps he had said them too often.

They were true words, too. That was the interesting thing about it.

What puzzles me is an old question. To tell the truth, how many men here in Marion are interested in automobiles? I mean really interested. Here is a machine closely interwoven into all of our modern life.

There is, however, no such relation between the men and the machine as there was formerly between the man and his horse. Many men seldom lift the hood of the machine they drive. There are delicate, strange things down in there. The motor is itself a strange thing, the differential, the apparatus for lighting the machine and the road.

It is all wonderful, strange. We take it all for granted. What is wrong is the very thing that makes it right, too. I mean that in perfecting modern industry man has simply got lost.

We all feel lost, too.

Formerly, at one time in my life, I had something to do with making motion pictures. No, I did not write for the movies. I had a job doing publicity for an actor. I never did much. I was put on the payroll and pretty much forgotten. At home I was at work on a novel.

I did, however, spend certain hours and days about the studios. It was a strange life. There were men and women there, acting in pictures the story of which they had never heard. They did individual scenes that were afterwards patched together to make the story in the office.

It is so in modern industry now. Formerly, at least, the whole machine was made in one factory. Now there is a system of factories, often in different towns. A great factory makes one part and another great factory another part.

Great assembly plants put the machines together. There is always this strange feeling of the separation of the man from the thing his hands make. It affects all life in a way few people realize. Much of the boredom of modern life is concerned in it. If there is any way out, any way to give back to the workman the feeling that here is a thing my own hands have made—a peculiarly healthy, satisfying feeling—I do not know what it is.

IN THE TOWN

September 20

Another term of court is drawing to a close. The writer dodges in and out of the courtroom. The little common dramas of everyday life are being fought out there.

There have been quarrels in families and neighborhoods. Life for most people is a hard, grim business. Hill men. Valley men.

Hard-working farm women.

Now in court everyone sits up. There is the question of the fatherhood of some fatherless child.

If the young man accused can prove that the girl has "stepped out," as we say, he can get out of it.

Other young men will come forward sometimes and give such testimony.

In the mind of the bystander pictures of country roads, fall evenings, spring evenings, summer evenings.

You will see groups of young country fellows, with their girls, on a country road of a summer night and hills, roads, and fields along the road.

A young couple loitering, falling behind the others. Over in Grayson they speak of such children as "woods children."

Some young country girls are cautious, determined, wary.

Others modest, shy, frightened.

Then there are the bold ones.

Life pulsating in all of them.

Being alone on a country road is quite a different matter from being in a courtroom.

Hatred, where there was once love. Someone is lying. Jaws are set. There is a hard look in the eyes.

You get life coming up to you like this, greeting you.

Horses shot in fields, an automobile stolen, liquor made and drunk.

Young men fighting in the road, stores and houses broken into and goods stolen.

It is the county prosecutor's business to prosecute. He stands as the spokesman of organized society.

"You have done this thing and you must pay the price."

"Stick it to them."

Other lawyers hired for the defense. The law is an attempt to arrive at justice. It is also a game. One side is trying to outwit the other.

The Smyth County juries strike the onlooker as peculiarly fair. They are not flip men. They try to arrive at justice.

Life is ruled by chance, too. Some are being tried for things you have done and you were never tried.

The boys and men who cannot get bail lie in jail. The jail is a terrible place. Sometimes men are sentenced to stay in there for six or eight months or a year.

Recently a young man came out. A friend saw him on the street. "Have you got a job?"

"Yes, but I cannot go to work yet. I have to walk about to get strength back into my legs."

Men weakened by long confinement in a close, unsanitary place. They come into court.

Some are lying, some telling the truth. The jury has to decide.

The prisoners are often a plucky lot. They go back to jail. In the jail all is excitement when court is in session. Men are going out of the jail into the court, going free or coming back for more long months of confinement.

Voices in there. "What did you get?"

"I got six months."

The men laugh. They take it with surprising courage. The writer never hears a sentence without a shudder shaking his whole body.

Not to be able to walk about, talk to people, see the stars, the sun going down.

Confined in the presence of others. Never to lose sight of them.

To have no solitude, to be unable to go alone into a room, close the door, stand there or kneel down.

Not to have books, clean clothes, a clean bed, a clean field in which to take an evening's walk.

It is education—here in Marion, being editor of the small town and county papers. Here I am closer to life than I have ever been.

The court, the field, the country road, the farmhouse, the street. It is a school when you have a definite place in it.

LATE SEPTEMBER DAYS

October 4

The children are going to school. Young men, too, and many handsome young women.

You get up in the morning shivering. It is time now for buckwheat cakes in the morning.

Always a touch of sadness at this time of the year. You hoped and planned so much for this year. "What, is another year going? What have I got done this year?"

On the hillside the maples are already turned or are turning. Veins of red, like blood, run through the leaves. Soon all the mountainsides will be glorious with color.

The people who come into our country for the summer lose the best and sweetest of it by going away too soon.

The corn-cutting is started. It is going to be heavy work in many parts of the country. The heavy rain and winds have got the corn down—a tangled mass.

Saw some fine corn on Bob McCarty's place, out on Highway Twelve.

After the corn is cut and in shock I always see it as an army standing in the fields—to drive away the grim wolves of want during the winter ahead.

The cold nights now make you sleep hard. In the morning the sun seems sleepy-headed. It does not want to get up.

ELECTION

October 4

To the editor every election is a miniature war. In any hard-fought election some of the same influences that are so apparent in times of war come to the front.

Men and women lose their dignity and judgment. Each side is intent on winning. Often it doesn't matter how they win. The end justifies the means, etc.

What was intended by man to be a process of selection of their governors, on merit, becomes a game, often merely a tricky game.

I often wonder how any man can bear to be in a high political

position, when it is so generally known what price has to be paid to
get there.

I have lived through two wars. During the great war I went
about praying always for the end of it. I look forward with pleasure
to the end of this political campaign.

Misrepresentations on all sides, lack of human dignity.

But I have no illusions that in what is called "the good old times"
it was any better. In the early days of our republic there was the
same thing going on. I have not read my history in vain. Bitterness
always—always ugliness when one party tries to defeat another.

Long rows of men who have been president and who, after being
president, have left no mark, nothing they can be remembered by.
The schoolteachers tell the children their names. Nothing remains
but a name on a long list of names.

No great achievement, nothing left of all the hard, bitter struggle
that once went on but a name on a list of names. It is hard work for
a sane man to see much sense in most of the election furor.

THANK YOU, LADIES AND GENTLEMEN

October 18

As almost everyone knows, when we took over the newspapers here, almost a year ago now, they had just been through a
hard-pounding circulation drive. Just as the drive ended, we bought
the papers. We have been delivering papers the subscription for
which was given to another man.

Hundreds of subscriptions expiring in August, September, October, and November. In fairness to all we decided we would not
keep on sending anyone the paper after the subscription time had

expired. We put the papers on a cash-in-advance basis and, after due notice, have taken off all names that did not resubscribe.

In order to get these renewals we have not put out any subscription agents.

However, the renewals have been pouring in. As many as ten, fifteen, and even twenty come in every day.

This is, as you may guess, tremendously flattering to your editor. It makes him happy, makes him feel good. We have been fighting to give a paper that was good reading, interesting, alive. We knew the test would come when people had to take it for another year. That they are taking it in greater numbers than ever and that many of them are kind enough to speak enthusiastically of it make us feel good clear down to our editorial toes.

MAMIE PALMER DIES

October 25

Our readers will remember Mamie Palmer, the bootleg queen. She was picked up on the highway near Saltville by sheriffs of the county with a load of liquor in her car.

When brought to Marion and sent before the Grand Jury, Mamie plead guilty and was put into our well-known jail. At once county health officer Ward, Judge Stewart, and others about the court interested themselves in Mamie. She was already far gone in consumption but was a cheerful soul. Everyone in jail liked the poor, thin woman with the sharp voice, the sharp tongue and eyes.

Whatever else she was, Mamie was a true stoic and a sport. She took it all, even her approaching death, as a part of life.

At once Judge Stewart wrote to Governor Byrd, telling of the dying woman's condition, and the governor pardoned her. Mamie was so evidently a woman who had been through a rough life, but many a woman in a good, comfortable home might have learned something from her. There is many a woman needs her spirit and her gameness.

We had written about Mamie in the papers and two men of Marion (names withheld on request) came in and asked us to see her and see if she needed money.

She didn't. There were West Virginia friends ready to take care of her.

They did try. But Mamie was too far gone. She went to her friends in West Virginia and was there for a week or two when she was taken with a hemorrhage and died.

THE DESPISED AND NEGLECTED

December 13

There is something that makes any man who has a bit of fame or notoriety puzzled all his life.

He begins getting letters from the despised, defeated, and neglected.

Well, what is he to do?

You take the matter of injustice, for example. Officers of the law go on the assumption that most men accused are guilty.

They are, too.

But there are men everywhere and women, too, who begin life defeated and despised and who remain defeated and despised always.

Something has got into such people. They are sure the cards are stacked against them and they are, too.

It is not easy to love or to like those who are not lovable and likeable.

You cannot give to those who will not receive.

Do you remember when you were a boy in school? There was always a boy all the rest struck or kicked.

There are little girls to whom the same thing happens.

They are ugly or think they are. Who knows what beauty in a woman is? Almost any woman becomes beautiful at moments.

You see love come to a plain girl. How it makes her eyes shine. She begins to walk with a new grace. Yesterday the girl or woman was plain, ugly—now she is lovely.

Everyone feels it. People make crude jokes about the love between men and women—it is the basis of endless vulgarity, but it is the one thing wanted, dreamed of.

We bow before the figure of Christ because he represents the spirit of inexhaustible love in the world, but at the same time we turn about and use all of our efforts to muddy love—to vulgarize it.

We despise what we are afraid to take.

Behold the painter who with his brushes and a few tubes of color makes a thing of lasting beauty, the musician who molds sounds into music, the sculptor who gives form and surface to stone.

These men are nothing but lovers.

But I am thinking now of the despised. I have a letter this morning from such a one. Many such letters come to me.

This letter is from a person to whom a terrible injustice has perhaps been done. He has been cast into prison. He has been kept there a long time.

At one time the whole country was interested in his case. He was a labor leader accused of murder. There was a question about his guilt.

The question was so serious that, at one time, the President of the United States interested himself in the man's behalf.

There was a flurry in the newspapers. Money was raised to fight the case.

He was not hung at last but he has been lying in prison for 13 years now.*

He writes to me out of his prison. "I am innocent," he says. "Help me get out."

---

* Thomas J. Zechariah (1882–1942), called Tom Mooney, was convicted of murder in 1917 and not pardoned until 1939.

But what can I do? I have no keys to his prison.

I tell you, if I had keys, at the Christmas time, I would open all doors to all prisons.

I would let them out—murderers, thieves, prostitutes.

But, you see, I am not in power. No one will ever put me into power. People in power would be afraid to give me keys to their prisons. They do right to be afraid. At any rate I have in me—somewhat—the power of love.

I am unashamed of it.

I would like to see all people be unashamed. I would like to see them walk proudly and gaily through the streets.

I would like them to love the ground under their feet, the air they breathe, their own bodies, the bodies of others.

There is a piece in our paper about a poor boy to whom an injustice was done.

There was a rich boy did the same thing and got off.

Well, it is so. Injustice of that kind is done constantly.

But do you think no injustice is done the rich?

The rich man may feel as deep a sense of injustice as the poor man.

I know a very rich man who wants the affection of men more than he wants anything else in this world. Wanting it, he constantly does things to hurt people, to make them despise him. He speaks proudly and arrogantly when he does not feel that way at all.

It is possible to be a rich man without a cent of money or a foot of lead.

It is possible to have thousands of acres of land and be poor and despised.

The world is no nearer understanding of love than when Christ walked here.

There are people to whom injustice will always be done. They are the neglected and despised. They carry their own prison within themselves.

Injustice is as much a part of human life as is the air we breathe, the ground under our feet.

There is no answer, no solution for the injustice of life. To think there is is to be a sentimental fool.

I am a man often proud and happy in life. I am rich in friends, in love. I like my food, my clothes, the air, the sky, the towns and cities.

But I know well enough that there are those who, from the cradle to the grave, must be neglected, defeated, and despised.

And I know there is often no justice that will make these people anything else.

They want what, if given them, they have no power to receive.

A STRANGER

December 20

First Andrew, the brown boy who sweeps out the shop, said he had been in and wanted to see me. "He is at the hotel and wants to see you bad," Andrew said.

He said it was Mr. Funk.

"Andy Funk?" I asked.

"Yes," Andrew said. Andrew isn't very accurate.

I was a little nervous, of course. Why should a prosecuting attorney want to see me in such a hurry?

Any officer of the law can scare me at any time by looking sharply at me.

I began to think of past sins. "Now what does that fellow know?" I ask myself. As it turned out, it wasn't Mr. Funk who wanted to see me at all. It was a stranger.

I had gone back to work in the office in the evening when he came in.

"May I see you? May I talk to you?"

"Why, yes. Why not?"

"It is some man who thinks he can write. He writes poems perhaps," I thought. I had an idea. I was tired and nervous anyway.

"Do you mind coming with me while I take a little walk?" I said.

It was, as I have said, night, and we walked out the highway to Henry Copenhaver's mill and back. Of course, we had to dodge cars all the way out and back. I hadn't looked at the man much in the office. In the light of the headlights of cars I looked more closely.

He was a sea captain. He told me that. He had driven down here from Norfolk. His boat, a freighter, was laid up for repairs. He said it would be there for some time.

He had a cousin living in Richmond and had gone to pay a visit. There he had borrowed his cousin's car. "I am just driving about the country," he said.

Well. And how did he happen to come to see me?

"I read a book of yours once," he said. "There was a story in it. It just happened to be my story.

"I do not mean my story as a sailor. It was before that, when I was a young man. The story was so exact. Something happened to me just like that. It was about a woman."

"Yes?"

"You see, it couldn't have happened to anyone else—just like that. You put everything down except the names. You changed the names, of course.

"I happened, you see, to hear that you were down here, in this part of the country."

"Yes?"

He told me the name of the story. We walked along in silence for a time.

"Well," I said, "I'll tell you this. As a matter of fact just the circumstances of that story happened to me, too. No one else. I put it down just as it happened to me."

"Do you mean it turned out for you just as it was told in the story?"

"Yes."

"It did for me, too," he said.

We walked along the road after that for a long time in the dark. We came to the lights of town. In front of the post office we parted.

Before we parted he asked me another question. "Look here," he said, "do you mind if I ask you another question?"

"Certainly not."

"Has anyone ever asked you before if that story was their story, too?"

"About a dozen men," I said.

He seemed surprised. He whistled softly. "Well, well," he said.

"It wouldn't have been a good story if it had not happened just like that to a lot of men," I said.

"Do you mean," he started to ask and then stopped. "Like that?

"Other women saying that same thing to other men under the same circumstances, eh?

"How many men do you suppose, in various places all over the world, are having the same thing happen to them, at just this moment?"

The idea that all lives are pretty much alike, that all people fall in love at some time, that they have times of illness and disappointment, times of joy, that they all finally get old and die seemed new to him.

I explained that the stories men tell are all old stories. "We only try to find new ways of telling them," I said. "The thing that happened to you, with that woman, has happened to thousands of men," I said.

The stranger said he had been to sea most of the time for the last twenty years. "Most of the time I have been an officer," he said. At sea an officer does not associate much with the men under him.

He seemed a little disappointed that the thing that had happened to him had happened to others. He had been through a certain experience with a woman. Perhaps the thought that other men had been through the same experience shocked him a little.

It made him feel less important perhaps.

I thought he went away from me with a look of disappointment on his face.

1929

EXPERIMENTAL LAND
EDUCATION

January 24

It is the man who knows nothing of writing who gives you most advice; the woman who has never had a child is most likely to speak or write about child raising; I think, in all fairness to them, that it will be admitted that most all the bitterness—well, say, against the old saloons—came from men and women who were never in a saloon.

Whether they were right or wrong is another matter. I am thinking of myself writing to farmers, trying to give them advice. The whole thing is a bit absurd.

I was born and raised in a small town, just such a town as Marion, Virginia. My father half ruined himself with drink. He had been born what he called "a gentleman" but had no head for business. Like myself he liked to take life with a certain flourish. I mean, to put the hat on the side rather than the top of the head, wear a loud tie, carry a walking stick.

Poor man, he never did get over loving women, and I dare say I never shall. When a woman makes herself beautiful I am grateful to her. I like to see her walking, beautifully gowned, through the streets. Really, I do not want her to pay any special attention to me.

I am grateful to her as I am grateful to the man who saved a lovely old building in a town, rather than tear it down to build an ugly although perhaps more efficient one.

I like men who are manly and frank, women who carry themselves with grace and beauty. My conception of what is nice in life is my own. I stand on it.

Only last Sunday I was walking in Marion with Mr. Funk. We passed two Negro children. They had nice faces and skins that would have made a painter mad with joy. O, the loveliness of the coppery browns and reds in the Negro children's faces. I have no way of knowing whether or not Mr. Funk saw what I saw. Probably not. I have thought about painting all my life. I wanted to be a painter but did not make it; so I became a scribbler.

My father's drinking made us poor, often we suffered extreme poverty; but afterward, a long time afterward, I did not blame him. Life was dull to him. Drink, I think, inflamed his imagination. He used to sing and tell marvelous stories to us children when he was drinking. Sober, he was often dull, sad, and heavy. In his cups he gathered us about his knees. He would read some old tale and expound it. He read us *Robinson Crusoe* and some of the Shakespeare comedies. He imagined himself Falstaff, although he was a lean not a fat man. He walked up and down the floor. There was no butter in the house. For weeks sometimes we lived on corn-meal mush. "Man does not live by bread alone," he said. It was hard on Mother, to be sure. We were, however, a family of boys. "Women do not understand the needs of us men," he said, with a flourish of his hand.

How many charming memories I have of the man. One night we went swimming in a pond. It was called Fenn's Pond and was at the edge of town. We went there on a rainy night.

So there we were at the pond's edge in the darkness. Black clouds raced across the sky. Father was a strong swimmer. "It is nice to swim naked," he said. "That is why I brought you here tonight."

"If you feel yourself tiring," said he, "put your hand on my shoulder."

And so, stripping ourselves and leaving our clothes on the bank in the rain, we plunged in. I remember his broad white shoulders, gleaming in the darkness, his strong man's arms flashing out. How small and weak my own arms seemed.

And now we had reached the farther shore and had drawn ourselves up on the wet grass. This was in the summer and the rain was warm. We lay there a long time.

In his grandiloquent way Father spoke of the sky. It was, I thought, very black, but we could see places where the black was denser. It stopped raining. "The sky is not black; it is deep purple," said my father.

He called attention to the deep purple of the water. Near the shore, where we were lying together, naked on the grass, it was actually black.

I remember also the lightning playing across the sky, the rumble of distant thunder.

Again I am a newsboy on the streets of our town. A strange lady, beautifully clad, has come to town. She is changing cars there, getting off a Lake-Shore and Michigan-Southern train to take the I. B. & W., later become the Big Four—a branch of that system.

I am a newsboy, a slip of a boy at the railroad station and there is that lady. My father comes into the railroad station, a little drunk. "Do you suppose she could be a princess?" I asked. Another man would have laughed at me but not Father. "I think very likely she is," he said. We walked together up and down the railroad station platform looking at the lady. He discovered a principality for her, I remember, in a strange, green land, far away overseas. There was a white castle on the side of a hill.

And so my father drank and we ate corn-meal mush, and Mother sorrowed often; but two of my brothers painted, and a sister, who later died, wrote sometimes rather delicate little verses that never got printed.

But what has all this to do with so high-sounding a title as "Experimental Land Education"?

Just this. I fell to thinking of my childhood, sitting in my little printshop in Marion, Virginia, and of the farmers who come in here. I was thinking of how, as a boy, I went often with my brothers to work on farms. We set out cabbage plants, acres of them, and later cut and hauled cabbage to market. We hoed, cut, and shucked corn; we picked strawberries in a strawberry field; cut firewood in the forest in the winter; helped to pick and pack apples in the fall.

I am thinking only that imagination can be applied to the land as well as to my own trade of writing.

Here we have politicians talking of "Farm Relief." Well! Farmers going on in a set way all their lives. They plant corn—if all their neighbors plant corn or cabbage or cotton. Once they begin to plant one crop they go on and on.

I think my own father did, for all his faults—of which I myself have more—teach his children a kind of self-reliance. "Use your imagination. Stand on your own feet." The very government, in helping you, may harm you.

"Trust God and give 'em Long Melford," said old George Borrow, a manly man who knew a lot. By "Long Melford" he meant an unexpected punch with the left.

And so I am thinking that every farmer should have on his farm a few experimental acres. He should talk these experimental acres over with his sons, with his hired men, as my father talked to me of the color of a night sky over Fenn's Pond in Ohio.

"We are raising corn, wheat, cotton, tobacco—what not. Let us set these few acres aside. We will play with them, experiment with them.

"We will throw manure on this land, plow it deep."

Why should every farm not be a college, too? O, the nonsense talked about education.

Books, books, I am weary of books. I am weary of the gabble of congressmen and presidents.

My own education was got on the farm, on the night streets of a town, in factories, with women I have loved. Nearly everything I have learned—and I have not learned much yet—has come by a thrust out into an experimental field.

For example, my running these country weekly papers in a Virginia town has been an experiment in my life. I do not know how much the people here have got from them but I have got a lot.

They have been experimental acres on the farm that is my life. I have plowed deep, put in this crop and that. I myself have never been much of a farmer but I have always loved the land. Many of my best friends are farmers. I think the modern age has sold the farmer out. The industrialists have got from government a lot; labor has got something; the farmer has got talk, nothing else.

I think he will continue to get—talk.

The farmer is an individualist, like the artist. His one chance, I believe, is in experimenting. As I have suggested, every farm should also be a college.

A few acres should be set aside each year for Experimental Land Education. It should be the land on which the imaginations of the farmer, his wife, his sons, his hired man are let loose, as my father let loose my imagination, swimming at night in Fenn's Pond and walking on a railroad station in a town in Ohio.

THE CRY FOR JUSTICE

January 31

It seems Mayor Maxwell and the town council recently went Bolshevik on roller-skating. Roller-skating became for the time and in the minds of the city fathers almost a capital offense. The Watkins boys had a roller-skating rink here. Where they came from, we don't know. They were tall young men who looked like mountain men to us. Had they confined themselves to roller-skating and raking in the shekels all might have been O.K.

But it seems they were up to other things—poker playing, for example. One of the Watkins boys got caught engaged in such a game.

This is said to have been the first poker game ever played in the history of Smyth County.

So Mr. Watkins was up before His Honor. "So-and-so many dollars and sixty days in jail," His Honor said, "and you don't need to go to jail if you close the skating rink, get out of town, and take your rink with you."

Which was all right and might have been justice. Justice is a thing we know little or nothing about. Often at night we awaken out of a deep sleep, trembling from head to foot, fearing justice may be done us.

But to return to our tale. Having soaked the Watkins boys, His Honor and the town council did not stop there. There was a called meeting of the council. They had all got afraid the Watkins boys might transfer their license to run a skating rink to someone else.

You see, there had been a slip-up when the Watkins boys got it too cheap. Who knew they were going to rake in all those shekels—who knew that our young blades and ladies were going to flit, night after night, through the mazes of joy—enticed by that tall Watkins who, heaven knows, could surely skate—who knew that nickels, dimes, quarters, and halves were to fall like gentle snowflakes into the Watkins' till?

Of course, no one knew.

The town, it seems, had gone skate mad. It was a disease, an epidemic. Much good silver was being diverted into these strange coffers, as one might say. Why, we even felt this bitterly ourselves. People who might well have been sitting at home, reading our papers and absorbing wisdom, light, and mental grace, were up there twining and intertwining themselves around that hall back of that long Watkins.

And to about the worst music we ever heard. We will say that.

We will say more. The town council said more. The special meeting was called by His Honor but His Honor was not there.

He was at home; he was sick; but his spirit reigned. The council said, first of all, that the Watkins' skating-rink license could not be transferred to anyone on the earth above the sea or to anyone in the waters under the sea.

But was justice thereby done?

Ah!

Let us examine and consider this matter. Let us walk under the night skies and think. We are strong for justice for everyone but ourselves. We do not want any justice in our own dish.

We don't want to roller-skate either. We never learned. We hate to fall down. We hate to have a certain part of our anatomy bruised. We hate to lose that grace people are accustomed to seeing in us.

But to return to Justice.

There are people involved in this whole matter who, by the action of our town council, are hurt, bruised, the joy of their lives taken away, their young hopes crushed.

For example, there is Colonel Stardust Collins.

Here is an exemplary young man, a bachelor—handsome, young, of unimpeachable character. He works in a bank and sleeps upstairs over the bank.

As anyone ought to know, working in a bank is confining; sleeping upstairs over a bank is confining.

A man needs exercise, he needs joy, association with his fellows, both male and female.

And so, for Colonel Stardust, the coming of the Watkins brothers was a joy. Who has not seen the Colonel, in the waning light of a summer evening, walking through the Rialto, his skates in his hand? Who has not seen him also in the stress and storm, as one might say, of winter evenings?

It is even said that the Colonel bought himself skates of silver, that he bought himself a season ticket. As a matter of fact, by this action of the town council and an irate mayor, he is out $23.00 and no cents.

But that is not all he is out. Colonel Stardust says—and we think he speaks with sage wisdom—that roller-skating never did bring a moral blight upon the souls thus engaged, least of all upon himself. He says that, as a matter of fact, it kept away sinful thoughts. "While skating," says the Colonel, "my mind was full not of sinful thoughts but of pure ones.

"I thought of birds mating in the spring, of sea gulls on lonely rocks in the ocean, of lambs gamboling on the green.

"Not gambling, you understand, with dice or cards, but with their legs—just as I skated."

And so the cry for justice goes up. We think the town council ought to give Jerry Collins his $23.00 and no cents. We think they ought to take the last, slightest insinuation of sinfulness, by thought or deed, off his name. We think they ought to backtrack this much.

The town thinks so; Wolfe's boarding house, where we eat, thinks so; the Rialto thinks so.

Will the town council act? That is the question.

If it is not done we think a mass meeting should be held.

WHAT SAY!

February 28

It is no doubt a notable drive. This writer has never driven through a more delectable land. For the procession of choice landscapes along the way, for color and land contour, there is not, I believe, a finer three or four hours' drive to be found in the country —at least, not that I have seen.

About Marion and all through Smyth County the hills have a soft, sensual quality. I drove to Roanoke recently, on a cold, gray January Sunday. There was that peculiar hushed, still Sunday feeling everyone knows. It could be felt on the road, in the towns, about farmhouses, and almost in the fields and woods. Everyone was indoors. Sunday dinners were on. You know how they eat in Smyth County.

I left Marion at noon and what few people I met on the road were in their Sunday best. As I got over toward Roanoke more cars appeared. The Sunday dinners were over. People were out for an afternoon's drive. Near Christiansburg, on a side road, a lover walked with his lady in the cold drizzle of rain. He had an umbrella in his hand but had forgotten to put it up. I didn't particularly blame him after I looked at his lady.

In one field the spring lambing had begun. There had been four lambs born, all black. I wondered if black lambs were more forward-looking than white ones. "I must ask Paul Bird about that," I thought. All four lambs were busily nursing.

I have been told, by Mr. Burt Dickinson (who next to Mr. Henry Staley is no doubt our best classicist), that in Smyth County the hills have a particular soft roundness because our country is so old. (Deep Sea Club, please take note of this.) It came up out of the sea earlier than most places in America. The land has had time to soften its outlines. As I have often said, it will become, some day, a painter's land.

Just this side the Reed Creek Bridge, and just beyond, as you go east, on top the two hills, the mountains in the foreground break away and you have a view of distant hills and mountains. It is breath-taking. I know of no better place on this drive to stop the car and fill yourself with the beauty of our country. Gray and tawny hills in these winter months. I thought of the view from the top of Iron Mountain, at the crossing of Smyth and Grayson Counties, where you look away into North Carolina.

O, the soft beauty of our Virginia landscapes, There are no such hills anywhere I have been, and where in America have I not seen them? When painters come into our land and begin to paint here I hope they will be good painters and not the sloppy, sentimental kind that spoil everything they touch.

Wytheville, with its wide Main Street, is an enticing town. There is always a peculiar air of leisureliness that comes from the sense of space. I dare say the citizens there are as alert as in any of our towns.

Christiansburg, in Montgomery County, is another lovely place but Pulaski is pretty bad. It seems rather a shame that all through traffic must go some seven or eight miles out of the way to pass through this town. The hills there are also not so inviting. They are more sharp and rugged. I suppose it is politics that takes us all around that long detour to get us east or west.

Pulaski itself given over to the factories. They protrude everywhere. The town a little makes the flesh quiver after the beauty of Smyth, Wythe, and Montgomery Counties. It is like being in some industrial suburb of Chicago. Gaunt, half-ruined mills are everywhere. The very ground is black.

Beyond Pulaski again the lovely soft hills. I like the red brick and the comfortable-looking white frame houses they build here in this section of Virginia. Usually they stand well back from the road with green and, in the winter, tawny-yellow fields between them and the highway. White farmhouses built clinging to the sides of hills are particularly nice. It was a painter who first called my attention to this. It would be hard, however, to find, in all America, a more charming country home than that of Oscar K. Harris, just east of Marion, that stands right out on the highway.

At one place on the drive to Roanoke you plunge abruptly down a winding hill and find yourself following a purple and gray river in a long horseshoe bend. It is a marvelous place.

Many breath-taking places during this drive. Hills and fields and houses and then more lovely hills.

At last Salem. It does not take long to get through Salem. It is a sad-looking town.

The factories and mills have not spoiled Roanoke yet. It is a hard town to spoil. A beautifully situated town, the Roanoke River, the hills, the pleasant valley in which the town stands. From your hotel bedroom window, provided you arrive before dark of a winter evening, as I did, and are fortunate enough to get a room far up and looking away to the west, as I did—and there is a smoky rain falling over the hills in the distance and the city streets. . . .

Providing all these things happen to you, as they did to me, you will stand a moment by the window looking out, and shake a bit with cold because you left the car door-slides open to miss nothing, and you will be glad, as I was, that fate has sent you to live in so gracious a country.

IMPRESSIONS OF AN INAUGURATION

March 7

I had got into Washington, from New York, in the morning. The railroad yards were filled with trains. Our train moved forward a few hundred yards at a time. At last we got in. I lost myself in the crowd.

The crowd was centered about Pennsylvania Avenue. All along the streets, wherever there was a few feet of vacant space, a stand with seats had been put up. The side streets, coming into Pennsylvania Avenue, were roped off. Enterprising men had built series of seats on trucks and had backed them into the street ends. The papers say there are 300,000 visitors in the city. How do the papers know such things? One paper says 150,000; another, 300,000. Evidently they do not know. There is a vast crowd.

The little stores along Pennsylvania Avenue, down toward the Capitol, have narrow windows facing the street. They have put two or three chairs for rent in each window.

They are all rented. Middle-aged women and girls sit in the chairs. They sit patiently for hours. Nothing happens. They look like wax figures. No woman can sit so, nowadays, without showing a great deal of leg. The legs are not particularly attractive.

It is a day when no pretty women are to be seen. It is odd about a man's reactions to pretty women. It may be that on some days all women look pretty, and even lovely, while on others they nearly all look rather sad. Well, they never do all look pretty.

I have been wandering about with friends. Among them is a fair Russian aristocrat. She is tall, strong, magnificent. I keep thinking of the old days in Russia, the days of Gogol and Turgenev and of the Russian grand dukes. This fair, tall Russian woman has what the painter Renoir was always speaking of as "a skin that takes the light." What a subject for a magnificent painting she would make.

She is speaking to me of the Americans in the crowd. She has lived a great deal in Europe. She says American crowds always impress her by their patience. "In Europe, on such an occasion," she says, "there would be all sorts of protesting organizations out marching.

"There would be the socialists, the anarchists, the labor people. They would march and shout; the police would rush upon them.

"At the same time there would be more gaiety. People would dress in brighter colors; they would dance and sing."

The Baroness has got an idea that the Americans have no nerves. "There are no neurotics here, are there?" she asks and I laugh.

I think of the queer little outbreaks of neuroticisms all about me everywhere I go, of my own neuroticism.

In a European city, on such a gala occasion, everyone would be sitting in comfortable chairs, in the sidewalk cafés. They would be drinking wine. There would be little or no drunkenness.

I see a good many drunken people in this crowd. Three drunken young men brush against me. They laugh. One of them says he slept the night before in a park in Washington. (It must have been cold sleeping.) Obviously, he is lying. I like imaginative liars. He says that during the night a squirrel bit him. The others in his party gather about me and laugh. They have all been bitten by the same squirrel. They can just stand on their legs. "You have got the squirrel in your pocket now," I suggest to the man who has addressed me. "Yes," he says. He invites me to go somewhere with him, to also be bitten by the same squirrel, but I decline.

Pennsylvania Avenue is a broad street. It runs straight down from the White House to the Capitol. Once it was lined with trees but there are no trees now. It is perhaps six times as wide as our Rialto in Marion. The street has been roped off with heavy wire ropes.

The politicians in their tall black hats have dull faces. The officers are wearing all of their medals. The breasts of some of the officers are loaded with decorations.

Most of the politicians have piggish-looking faces. They are amazingly fat.

I have followed the crowd and have gone to see the inauguration. The skies are gray and cold. Mr. Hoover and Mr. Coolidge have gone to the Capitol in a slowly moving car. Mr. Coolidge looks happy. They bow to the right and left. Walking beside me is a man in a hunter's jacket and a coonskin cap. He tells me he is impersonating Daniel Boone for the Governor of Pennsylvania. We pass a statue of General Grant and talk about him. "He was a good man, all right," the Pennsylvania Daniel Boone says.

In the Capitol grounds a vast crowd has gathered. We cannot hear the words of the new President. He is talking about prohibition, as we learn later from the newspapers. Near me a political marching club is passing a bottle of whiskey from hand to hand. They drink openly, without attempt at concealment. They also are from Pennsylvania.

It has begun to rain now and, although the crowd stands patiently in the rain. hearing nothing, I go away. I have lunch in a

side street, away from the crowd. When I come back the bands, the
sailors, the soldiers, the marching clubs—all their gay feathers
drooping—are marching patiently. It rains harder and harder. Four
huge blimps float in the air above. They nose their way slowly
through the mist. The crowd sit patiently in the rain. I hear no
cheers, although tomorrow the newspapers will speak of the "cheer-
ing crowds."

As there is no other place to get dry and as my friends have long
since gone home, I go to a movie house. It is the only place I can
find to sit down.

On the screen they are showing the ideal American woman. She
is called "Miss America." She spends the whole day putting on and
taking off expensive clothes. We see her in bed, in her bedroom, at
tea, at the theater. She wears pajamas, tea gowns, bathing suits,
party gowns without number. The women in the theater watch her
breathlessly. Their eyes are filled with envy.

When I come out of the theater the parade is over. It still rains.
The new President has gone to his home in the White House. The
Washington newspapers take a great amount of space to tell about
the gowns worn by the various wives of the new men, just come
into power.

P.S. I am at the railroad station, waiting for my train home. It is
two hours late. I have dined with my friends. At the station are
many military companies. Bands are playing.

A man comes to me and talks about Virginia in the parade.
"Virginia was great," he says. "Did you see the Richmond Blues?"
Alas, I did not. They must have been parading as I sat in the movie
theater watching Miss America put on and take off clothes.

At the station the band plays a dance tune. People begin to
dance. An impromptu dance is organized. I join in. I dance gaily
about with a lady who tells me she is studying painting in New
York. She is a handsome lady. Another lady tells me of a son about
to be christened. She asks me if I will come to the christening and I
say I will. I will go, too. Who knows, perhaps she will name the
child for me.

A TRAVELER'S NOTES

March 28

I have always been a passionate traveler. I love the fields, the streets of my town (in the daytime and at night), the creeks and rivers, the clear blue of our Southwestern Virginia skies, the roads with the flying automobiles, the cattle in the pastures.

But.

The city ache comes to me. I begin to want New York.

I want to go into the studio of the musician. He will talk to me of music, stopping now and then to go to his piano to run his fingers over the keys. It is thus he illuminates his talk. The world of sound is again open to me. This is not the radio, howling in the quiet night or the dreadful false voices of politicians or of an announcer speaking off an advertisement of spark plugs.

The man with whom I am now sitting is touching to life before me the world of delicate, colorful sounds that have come into his consciousness and now come into mine. Words become inadequate to express his thoughts. He goes to the piano to tell me in sounds what he cannot put into words.

Or I have gone to the painter. I shall be fortunate if I find him at work.

If he will let me, I shall take a book and sit quietly in a corner of his studio.

"Work on. Only let me sit here."

The painter is after some difficult thing. There is life in painting again nowadays. As in writing prose, few enough men succeed but many are trying.

They have "since Cézanne lived," they all say (and it must be true), a new sense of color in life. The backgrounds of paintings are not dead now. Even at this minute, as I sit writing, I am in the house of a painter in a suburb twenty miles from New York. It is an old house on a side street of an old town. The sun is shining outside. Through a window I can see the warm, yellow sunlight on an old stone wall. I hear the man's wife moving about the house. He is a man past fifty who has got him a young wife.

The man in his studio nearby tacking canvas on a frame for a new painting. A half hour ago he was talking to me of what he hopes to do with this canvas. I had been down to the main street of the town and had brought him back a bunch of yellow flowers, and he wants to paint them. Already he has made a sketch.

The flowers will stand in a vase, the light streaming in on them from a window.

It is one thing to conceive of such a painting and another to realize it. The painter knows that and I know. The drawing he has already made is nothing.

"Everything is color," he said, going out of the room where he has left me sitting in order that I may write of my adventures here in this world of artists.

He has, however, left some paintings for me to look at as I write.

There is one of a nude woman lying on grass beside a stream. The artist attempted something very difficult in this canvas. There is a boat nearby. The woman has been bathing. She has taken brightly colored cushions from the boat and thrown them on the grass.

No one is near. She lies there, her eyes looking off into the distance. Her arms are thrown above her head.

The warm flesh is lovely against the green.

A tree nearby is much alive. It is all tree as the woman is all woman.

At the brook's edge are some silvery stones and the boat on the river is gray.

The painter is trying to make color and light sing across his canvas as the musician tried to make sounds sing and as I try sometimes to make words sing and rattle and cry out on my pages.

And so seldom succeed.

There is this world of these artists and it is aside from the world in which much of my life is spent, but how I love to come occasionally among them as I am doing now. As I am a writer, writing of people, I must spend much of my life buried in the ordinary life of people.

But, O, how I love to hear the sincere, inquiring painter talk of his light, his colors, his masses of solids. When I go back to my own hills, I shall see them in a new and more vivid way for being here in this room.

There is another painting. A cat is lying stretched out among soft, colorful cushions.

But I will not speak more of these paintings now. The painter's wife has just come into the room looking for a workbasket she left here.

Her coming diverts my thoughts. In a nearby yard children are crying to one another with their sharp little voices. An early spring wind is racing through bare branches of the tree outside the windows.

Again I think of the musician's world and of my own world.

Color, light, sound, the shapes of things.

People.

To go, as I do, into the painter's world, into the world of the musician or the sculptor is a voyage into a delightful foreign country.

In a distant part of the house I hear the voice of the painter's wife explaining something to him.

"My dear, when I spoke sharply to you, when you were impatient for your breakfast, I was not really in a bad humor. I loved you then and I love you now."

"Well, go away, my dear. I am thinking about painting now. I am not thinking about love."

I do not think of love, looking at the woman on the grass. I think of lovely warm colors in flesh, of the strangeness and wonder of the human form.

I think of the hills of my own country and how, sometimes, when I walk or ride among them, they are like lovely women.

I think of men ploughing in fields, of the breasts of horses as they come toward me along the furrows. I think of the sounds made by our Virginia streams, rolling and tumbling over rocks.

I think of men meeting and talking, of men riding in automobiles, of lawyers, doctors, farmers, laborers.

A procession of figures floats through my mind.

I am everyone else in America. I am always wanting to do something big. Only yesterday I walked in the streets of New York thinking of a great novel I might someday write.

I wanted to be a Zola, a Hugo, a Balzac.

What nonsensical thoughts I had.

Why am I not content to be small?

Yesterday was a warm, true day to me and everything I did all day was small and of no importance.

I had got to the city two or three days before and had gone to see two or three friends.

Then I had walked in the streets and had ridden in the subway. I was feeling the city hunger in me.

I went farther uptown. A bridge is being built that will span the Hudson River.

I went into a vacant lot overlooking the river and a ferry and, sitting on a stone, wrote some letters. I wrote to my son, "Send me such and such a book."

Then I wrote to a beloved man. "I would you were here, sitting beside me on this stone," I wrote.

Some boys were playing ball nearby. Once a batted ball whizzed past my nose. "How strange that I could be in my own quiet country fishing beside a stream with Pat Collins but a day or two ago and now here," I thought. I knew no one of all the thousands of people passing in the street nearby. The sun shone warmly on the face of the river. Tugs were passing, There were great barges loaded with timbers.

I went down off the ferry to where lumber was being taken off a barge and loaded on trucks. There was a man with a fish pole. He was not fishing. At once he told me he had never in his life owned a fish pole until the day before. Then he had seen a man casting a fly in a fly-casting contest in a park.

"I thought I would like to try it," he said.

"Well, it is a delicate art. If my friend Burt Dickinson were here, he could show you more than I can.

"You take it like this—see? I have seen my friend do it.

"You whip it out, so."

"The man in the park did it like that but he did it better than you do."

There were three men seriously fishing nearby. I went to speak to them. They were all old men. "What kind of fish do you catch here?" I asked.

"We catch tommies," said one of the men.

"And what kind of fish are they?"

"They are a fish that are sometimes that long" (holding his hands apart).

There was the one old man of the party who had a sour face. He was a misanthrope. His eyes were gray and dead. The lines about his mouth were set and determined.

"Tommies are not that long; they are never that long," he said with cold determination. "They are only as long as the span of your hand."

"I tell you they are sometimes a foot long."

"They are not."

"They are."

"They are not, I tell you."

"They are."

"They are not. They are the span of my hand."

"Only last Saturday I saw a man catch a tommie here. It was a foot long. You know the man; he has a store over there."

The man was pointing to a store on a nearby street.

"They are the span of my hand."

And now two of the old men had become angry. One of them walked with a determined air along the dock and across the street.

He had gone to the store to get the man who had caught the fish.

The man came back with him. He was a large man, evidently a butcher, and wore a white apron. Also, he had a red neck and large, quiet, blue eyes.

"Listen now, you, listen. Did you not, last Saturday, catch here a tommie a foot, twelve inches, long?"

"I did.

"I was not fishing myself. I walked along here, along this dock. There was a man fishing here, a man I knew.

"Our store is open on Saturday afternoon but I had been out to lunch.

"The strange thing was the man's line did not jerk. It was taut enough.

"I was only fooling. 'Jim,' I said, 'I will catch you a fish.'

"I pulled in his line. There was a tommie on it. It was twelve inches long."

"Tommies do not grow so large," said the sour old man sitting on the edge of the dock. His eyes were as impersonal as the sky. How cold and determined the lines of his mouth.

The three other old men on the dock were furious. They threw up their hands in disgust and walked away.

"Tommies are little things," said the misanthrope, looking up at me. He held out a withered hand. "They are no larger than the span of my hand," he said, looking away over the river.

A TRAVELER'S NOTES

April 4

For the provincial, coming to New York as I do for a few weeks at a time, the soil of the country clinging to him, remembering fields and open places, there is always the excitement of the crowded streets. How fine to walk on Fifth Avenue in the late afternoon, seeing the beautiful, expensive cars, the shops, the well-dressed, fashionable women.

Then there are the great hotels, the theaters, the crowds about the theaters late at night.

Near the hotels, often in the lobbies, are the offices of brokers. During the day, the women speculators sit intent, watching the figures on the boards. Most of the women are fat, with stupid faces.

It is something also to go to the water front to see the ships leaving. A friend is leaving for Europe. I go to the boat to see him off. At night from my hotel room I hear the hoarse bawling of incoming and outgoing steamers.

There is, however, another side to all of this life of the city. I remember and go far downtown in the late afternoon. The day's business in the city is over now. I am caught up by the home-going crowd.

A cry within me—"How did I escape? What divine accident of

life has set me free of this?" Once I also was caught in the modern city business rush. I have never been able to grow rich by my writing. If I had not escaped to the country, perhaps I would still be here, a slave to the time clock in one of the great office buildings.

I have gone far downtown in New York to ride the subways uptown at the rush hour.

I have come out of a street where thousands—men and women—are pouring out of the great buildings. They come faster and faster, more and more thousands. The sidewalks of the narrow streets are inadequate. The roadways are jammed.

There are men of all ages, women of all ages. However, most of the people of the crowd are young. Boys run shouting among them. All grab at newspapers. The faces of the young men all seem prematurely old. There is weariness in the eyes. I sense something like premature senility.

The young women also have weary eyes. The painted mouths are already becoming slack. The mouths droop at the corners.

This is in the great financial district of New York. This is where the great modern industries are organized and controlled. As the newspapers so love to say, "Big things are done here." The streets are not streets but canyons. For far up there is a streak of light, delicate blue—the sky. The skies over New York are amazingly delicate in hue. If you look up, in this street at this hour, you will be pushed and shoved, perhaps knocked down.

I am in the street at this hour and hurry forward with the crowd. As I am pushed and shoved forward, I look about me.

These people have been compiling figures all day. They have been preparing figures, reports, for the great financial and industrial magnates. None of them know anything about the figures they have been working among. Only yesterday I talked to a woman who works down here in one of the great banks.

"Everything is more hurried and more senseless every year," she said bitterly. How tired and resentful the woman's eyes were. "Everywhere I read of the efficiency and humanness of modern business, but it is all a lie," she said.

"It is efficient for one purpose—to pile up more and more money for those who already have too much. The common man and woman has got lost.

"There is no place for us in all this," the woman said. "It does not take us into account. We know nothing of what we are doing. They do not want us to know.

"Everything possible is done to separate us from each other. Even the old feeling of union we used to have, in doing together a task we more or less understood, is being lost.

"Everything is being done more and more hurriedly, more and more cheaply." She explained to me that it was the aim of all modern industry to make the individual of less and less importance as an individual. The thing to do is to so arrange things that no one is indispensable. Everything is system, system. "Write these figures on these cards; add them up on that machine. Put them in this box. Faster, faster, faster."

"But what are the figures about?"

"I do not know. Do it faster, faster, faster."

In the great department stores, another sort of thing is going on. The clerks are also being made of less and less importance. Even to be polite to the buyer is not of the importance it once was. People do not want politeness. They want speed and low prices.

"Chuck things at them. Hurry up. Hurry up."

"It would be a good thing to smile. You do not need to feel like smiling. The movies will show you how it is done. Look at the pictures of the politicians. They are always smiling."

"Make life more and more impersonal. To be personal is dangerous. Human feelings come in."

Even the retail stores are all owned in chains now; the newspapers are owned in chains.

The newspapers all have the same tone. There is something sacred about business. "Government is business," said Mr. Coolidge. Once it was thought that government was intended to do something for the lives of all these nameless people. Business was of very secondary importance to the early Americans. It was thought to be rather vulgar.

See the big, bright, beautiful businessman at the top now. When he has got a great deal of money he will endow a college. Isn't it all quite perfect?

In the meantime these growing thousands of submerged ones, without meaning in their lives, with no direct connection with the work by which they live. They are being packed more and more closely in the great industrial centers.

They are pushed and shoved about like cattle. In this home-ward-bound city subway crowd some try to protect themselves while others are carried along like bits of driftwood in a flood.

Those who protest are pushed aside. "Get out of the way." I see a young woman thus pushed aside by a strong man. She is angry and clenches her fists. "God damn you," she cries. The man pays no attention. He pushes another woman aside and goes on.

How ineffectual even the woman's profanity. No one listens.

I have joined this homeward-bound subway crowd for my soul's good. I am seeing another side of city life here. Yesterday I walked on Fifth Avenue, dined with a rich gentlewoman; now I am here.

I am swept down a hole in the street and into a subway train. It is fortunate my coat is not torn. There are ten times too many people in the car in which I find myself and more will push and shove their way in at every station. Long since, all the seats have been taken. The air is rank.

We stop at other stations. More and more people are packed in. Bodies meet in close, terrible embrace.

In these subways the weak and defenseless are at the mercy of the strong and brutal. Any young woman compelled to work down-town in New York, who must habitually use the subways at the rush hours, can tell you stories of the things done to her by men in the jam. Bodies are pressed together. It is impossible to move, to escape.

Year after year it grows worse. The modern cities are not being run for the comfort of these millions. They are the nameless ones, the sheep, the workers, the clerks. Nowadays they are paid well enough. People in the crowd are surprisingly well dressed.

There is, however, a deep, underlying dissatisfaction. These peo-ple have nothing to do with the work they do, with the cities they live in. They are of no importance. They are automatons. Life pushes and hauls them, shoving them here and there. They feel themselves giving their lives to nothing. How dull the faces are. When the subway has got far uptown, the crowd begins to thin. Newspapers are taken out. Dull eyes look at the pages.

Most of the newspapers being read by this crowd are of the

cheap picture sort. They are altogether vulgar and horrible. Is it any wonder that dull lives, so fed, crowded into these places so, take ugly turns? The men in the crowd take it out on the women. They go as far as they dare.

And every night and morning the same thing happens. Riding with this crowd, my own personal dignity has been swept aside. I have been insulted, pushed, and hauled, and I am not a young girl. I am a strong man. Now I feel a driven pig.

At last I get out of the subway far uptown. I am in a street of huge, cheap apartment buildings. Clerks, laborers, stenographers, who have been riding with me in the subway, are diving into holes in the great cliff-like buildings. Families live in two or three rooms. Here they must love, eat, and sleep. Children are born and grow to manhood and womanhood here. What can the man or woman so hauled and pushed, so insulted, bring into a house?

I walk for a long time in such streets. Now most of the families have had their evening meal. Radios are turned on. From all sides voices. The voices coming over the radio are all telling the people of the wonder and glory of this modern life of ours. How long do you think they will go on believing?

SPRING

April 11

It is in the air. The hand of God has touched again the fields, the hill, the forests. In the forests you have to look closely to see anything.

It is there, however. How glorious it would be to live among a people who really saw God in nature and did not spend so much time making pretence.

For example, a town and a county like this should have a spring festival. It should not be held to raise money for any club, an organization of this kind. Children should go through the streets singing. There should be dances, not in stuffy halls but out of doors. Men and women should go about greeting each other. Wrongs done one another should be forgotten and forgiven. Now there should be no sinners and no good people.

Even if we poor CIVILIZED people must always be thinking of those cold sisters of Philistia, money and morals, it is too bad we cannot realize how little joy costs. The money spent for bad whiskey in this county would pay for a splendid spring and fall festival.

Is it any wonder that sensitive men (artists) who go to visit savage races come away often feeling they are better and more religious people than we who call ourselves civilized? I remember that Herman Melville, an early American writer and a true man, was once lost for some months among a race of so-called "savages" in the South Seas. If he was not so lost in fact, he was in fancy. The experience is recorded in a notable book called *Typee*. The man lived for some months among cannibals.

He found them the most gentle people in the world. They were aware of nature, skies, winds, rains, the fields, the forests.

I have just returned to my own country from a visit to the East. I spent most of my time there among young painters. Such men are good for me; they cure me of the disease of living.

It is because they are awake to things in nature that, for a large part of my own life, I did not see. I was too much absorbed in trying to get on, to succeed.

It is so also with most of the successful men of the arts I used to go to see. I mean the successful story writers, novel writers, painters, musicians. These men are always concerned with the question of how many books they will sell, with the question of how their paintings will sell.

They talk like stock brokers.

Often I wish that simple people could quit honoring these men. I wish they would quit honoring successful politicians and other public men. I wish they would honor themselves.

This morning I looked out my window and there was a man spading to make a garden. As he bent over, lifting the spadefulls and turning them over, I saw his task as a ceremony, a kind of morning prayer in the morning of the year.

I see all men doing simple tasks so.

I have been up the road toward Wytheville and have seen the farmers in their fields plowing. I am glad that, in spite of the greater wages to be made in towns and cities, men stick to the farms. I only wish men would sing more as they plowed, that they would feel pride and joy in these simple, direct tasks that keep them close to nature.

The muscles in the bodies of the horses are singing now. Why should men and women not sing, why should they not dance with joy because the spring has come again?

All of nature is dancing. See the trees scattering their blossoms in the wind. Listen closely. You will hear the singing of the plow in the furrow. The leaves dance as they unfold.

It is only man who will not unfold. He remains tight, stupid, in the spring. Even his religion is a sad thing. He does not dare have joy in it. "That is of the flesh," he says. He is afraid of his own flesh. "Flesh is of the devil," he says. As well say the trees, the blossoms coming now on trees, the earth itself is of the devil. It is all flesh.

O, the fears of men, the tightness of men. In the spring too many of us are in houses, poisoning each other with thoughts, instead of being outdoors and being cured.

Now the fields are being plowed. What a glorious thing is the plowed field. A fragrance arises from it. The soil is of many colors in our country. A plowed field is like a lovely painting.

In the city when I recently visited there, I went to see rich men. There was a man I used to know when we were both boys. He has got rich so that he does not have to work anymore. Most of the rich men I know are sick men.

"I have plenty of money. I do not need to work now."

"What do you do with yourself?"

"I fool a little with the stock exchange."

He does more than that. He runs from one expensive doctor to another, trying to buy health. Once, when we were both young fellows, he loved music but he has forgotten that now. He is a sick, successful man and will make others about him sick until he dies.

At another place I walked with two young writers under one of the most lovely night skies I have ever seen. They talked of nothing but the difficulty of making money by their writing. They did not call it "money making." They cried out for what they called "recognition."

The point is that, as we walked, they did not see the loveliness of the sky over their heads. Again and again I called attention to it but they could not see. They were blinded by the desire to succeed.

Well, the spring is here. It is for those who will and can see and feel it. On all sides nature is making lovely pictures now. The scene changes from day to day. It would be good if we could all dance now, if we could all sing.

HOW MANY MORE SPRINGS?

April 18

This whole country is lovely now. It is hard to stay in the printshop. Every day this editor has a new love. Well, there is Jack Sheffey's orchard. The editor has been up on cemetery hill to see it in all kinds of lights. The best place is from the road through the cemetery, around the crest of the hill. (Incidentally, there are few more lovely spots in this world in which to take the long adventure of death than the cemetery at Marion.)

From the hill the whole orchard—two orchards, really—can be seen. The road goes away into the distance and is lost among hills. Someday, if Marion ever has a sudden growth, this should be a charming residence section. To sit up there, in the rain, in the sunshine, in the gray mist, looking at the lovely valley, at the flowering trees, at the hills in the distance, is an experience not to be forgotten in this life.

How many more springs?

Drive out the Lyon's Gap road almost to the top of the pass. As you go toward Saltville the Holston Valley opens out to the left. There is the Whitetop in the distance. All that lovely country from Seven Mile Ford down to Chilhowie laid out before you like a floor.

To the top of Walker Mountain on Sunday evening. O, that I had been a singer there. The whole of the Holston Valley can be seen from up there. On Sunday evening banks of dark clouds arose above Whitetop and above Brushy and Iron Mountains in the distance. The clouds continued the theme of the land and the mountains.

The light was very clear. As darkness came on, the light over the scene changed constantly. I had engaged myself to dinner in town but forgot about it.

On the side of the mountains the dogwood. They are like flocks of sheep.

Behold, thou art fair, my beloved; behold, thou art fair; thou hast doves' eyes within thy locks: thy hair is like a flock of goats, that appear from Mount Gilead.

Thy teeth are like a flock of sheep that are even shorn, which came up from the washing; whereof everyone bear twins, and none is barren among them. [Paraphrased from the Song of Solomon.]

The road through Possum Hollow now, Mr. Bonham's Orchards on both sides of the road, toward Troutdale, the road down through St. Clair Bottoms. The road to Wytheville. Went there on Tuesday evening to dine with Mr. Powell Chapman. Left him at ten-thirty. A bleak, cold wind blowing.

It sang about the car. The apple blossoms were blown like snow in the light of the car ahead all the way home.

Every hour or two the sun looks out.

Now I am glad I am a country man. It seems to me sometimes that God will never forgive those who are cooped up in cities these spring days, in these days of the year's passion.

How many more springs? Many, many more for this poor sinner, he hopes.

THE MOMENT

June 20

Every dog has his day. Every year has its day, too. There are special fall days, spring, summer, and winter days.

Here we are, knee-deep in June. It must be that I am losing my youth. Nowadays people are rarely as satisfactory to me as are the fields and forests. It goes without saying that I am rarely satisfied with myself. It takes a deal of faith to get much out of people. Understanding is too rare a thing.

When the winter has passed, I remember always one day, one hour. Last winter it was a stormy day in New York. I rode for hours in a taxi with a dear friend. The storm howled about us. I remember the motors, jammed at the street crossings, the people hurrying, heads downward, through the storm.

Sense of the great city, the power of man, and the power of nature.

Last fall it was a day on Iron Mountain. Never was there another country like this for fall days. The whole world was awash with color that day. I sat in my car, on the top of Iron Mountain (you can see far away into the hills of North Carolina from up there). Toward Marion I looked off into the Hurricane.

Without a doubt man got the idea that led to the making of beautiful carpets from the fall forests, touched with frost, just as he got the Gothic from the tall aisles of trees in the forest. The forests are the fathers of the cathedrals. Who can doubt that?

The summer is something else. This year I got my day, my hour, in the town itself. It swept over me like a new love—as though I had seen for the first time some lovely woman I would remember as long as I lived.

I was sitting before a house. What views we have from the porches of houses here. Almost every house in Marion has a magnificent view.

There are glimpses of forests and orchards, towering hills. From the new golf clubhouse in Marion there is a view that would drive a painter mad.

It is so from the porches of scores of houses here. A curse upon that our printshop is stuck down in a hole, facing the town jail. If we did not have the little park here, it would be the most dismal spot in town.

For every man and every woman a day, an hour, when he is most manly or she most beautiful. All of life may feed into that hour as all the life of a rosebush into one hour. There is a day when the grass in the meadow and the wheat and corn in the field are most lush, most alive.

A day for the garden and the orchard, a fall day, a summer day. Watch out for it. It is near at hand, the richest, ripest day of the summer.

Every dog has his day.

RESPONSE

July 18

The life of the modern writer, like that of the modern painter or singer, is strange and different. To the normal man, to work is to live. In work there should be laughter, the dance, sadness, the expression of all of a man's feeling for all life.

It is difficult to get these things—a man's self—into any sort of work now. Modern life fights a man. In the attempt to conquer nature, man has not got so far.

Nature goes far off; it laughs at him; it remains untouched, unconquered.

The writer seeks to draw close. He loves, he marries, has children. Modern life tugs and hauls at him.

Money is everything to the artist. Who loves luxuries as he does?

"Very well, you may have money," the world says. "Come into the factories."

All the modern ways by which the artist in prose gets money take on the aspects of factory labor. Everything is forced into a mold, is standardized.

I am a man who has tried to escape. It has been a game. Publishing a newspaper has been but one turn of the game I have tried to play with life.

Running a country newspaper is one thing, one attempt. Tomorrow I may try something else. In a country newspaper office I have had real moments.

Other moments in a hall where laboring men were organizing.

Moments in city streets, at ball games, in the presence of the work of painters.

In halls where music was being played.

A man's contact with nature—in fields, skies, men, houses, cities—gets lost. He becomes, in a queer way, vile.

He is depressed, unhappy.

I remember moments when I was desperate to the point of attempted suicide.

Then—

Perhaps I was walking in the fields at the edge of a town. I stopped under a tree. "On the limb of this tree I could hang myself."

Well, a bird darts out of a bush; a man with a team goes to a distant field.

Such a man as I am stands trembling. Words again begin to dance in his head. He lives. The world becomes alive again. He loves life.

There is some chance yet—the arrangement of words in sentences—gaily, sadly, boisterously, with laughter on the lips, in the heart.

Perhaps I shall yet write some few more sentences that mean something real, that sing, that dance. . . .

With laughter buried deep down in them, too—the laughter that is real, that so few in this world ever understand enough to find.

There is a sun shining, rivers running. . . . Trees grow on hillsides. A man does not amount to much. A man is everything. To develop his own idiosyncrasies, his own moods, to dare to attempt to live, in nature, in art. . . .

To draw a little close again to nature—to be humble before nature.

You see the man walking gaily out from under the tree. That is the story. Laugh if you can. He has not hanged himself.

COME IN

December 5

The clerk's office, in the courthouse, is the great conversational center of Marion. There you may get almost any sort of conversation at most any time of the day.

There are two large rooms. To the room to the west Mr. Herbert retires when there is work to be done. Miss Elizabeth Brockman works there in the morning.

In both rooms there are large tables and comfortable chairs, and Mr. Sam Kent is usually to be found in the east room.

The county officials come in and go out. There is Sam Dillard, Sir Oliver, Hi Whistman, Si Price of Chilhowie (often seen with the famous Black Cat in his arms), Jim Carter, George Gullion, Squire Farris, and others.

People are coming in and going out. At this season of the year and in the spring, when the fishing starts, a good many men are coming in to get fishing and hunting licenses. There are awkward farm boys, tall, mature farmers in boots, young town sports. Two boys come in with a little paper bag in which are hawks' heads. The county pays a bounty for these. Often they are old and somewhat ripe. A faint, rancid odor pervades the room.

The room is a great gathering place for lawyers and they often have business there. Records of land sales, mortgages, etc., are to be looked up. Often clerks drop in from the banks. They are looking up the titles to lands on which applications for loans have been made.

Mr. Herbert Kent, who attends to everything and who has a reputation for accuracy, is one of the sort of workers who works without fuss. He goes quietly about. Men come to him about questions of law. The Code of Virginia is fairly at his tongue's end. Often there will be a discussion regarding some obscure point of law. "It is so and so."

"No, you are wrong about that."

The Code is brought out. In a surprising number of cases Mr. Herbert is right.

During the year almost every man in the county has business of some sort in these rooms.

It is the great conversational center of Marion. In the cold winter the Senate, at the back of City Drug, passes upon the more serious questions of state and town, but at the clerk's office all conversation takes a more general turn.

This is your place for anecdotes, for reports of crops and hunting, for county history, records of families. . . .

"Do you remember Jake?"

"Yes, where is he now?"

"Well, he went to Kansas."

"To what family did he belong?"

The record of Jake's family is gone into. You can find out when the family came into this country and where they came from. In nearly every old family there are a few queer characters. Tales are told of these.

The lawyers also are great story tellers. This is the sort of assembly on which Abe Lincoln practiced. Queer old court cases are gone over again. One story leads to another. The conversation goes on all day long.

And this is very distinctly a male assembly, too. It is true that occasionally a couple come in about a marriage license. They are embarrassed. They stand in the outer room whispering together.

Then the young man comes in. He looks furtively about. It may be that he does not know Mr. Herbert. He approaches the wrong man but is set straight.

Often the marriage ceremony is held right there, in the west room, the door having been closed. The men in the outer room become silent. They are perhaps remembering their own marriage day. "Did I make a mistake or didn't I? If I had it to do over again, would I do it?" *

Questions in men's eyes. A minister has been sent for or the ceremony is performed by a squire.

Well, that's done. Another family has been launched in the county. The young couple go away. The older men sitting about wish they were young again.

The best time in the room is the late afternoon. The windows look out upon the Rialto. Now it is five o'clock. Boys are playing ball or, in the fall and winter, football in the yard outside. People are going from the factories or stores, homeward bound. Any man passing along the street outside may give a turn to the conversation.

At this time of the day you are likely to see in the room any of the following men: Mr. Bob Goolsby, George Cook, Bill Birchfield, Jack Sheffey, Jim White Sheffey, Preston Collins, Jim Arney, Sam Dillard, Charles Funk, Burt Dickinson, sometimes Doctor Dave.

These are fairly regular attendants. Many others come occasionally.

At these gatherings almost any subject may get to the front. There are questions of government, labor, industry, improvements in the town, marriage, morality, crime, the past, the future.

And so the question of education is to the fore.

"Who is the best-educated man or woman in this town? Those present are excluded, of course."

A well-known woman is named. "I tell you, she is smart. She knows a lot. She can talk on almost any subject."

"Yes, she can talk, but what does she say?"

"It is a question of what education is." There may be a long discussion on this point.

"If you take education as a matter of book knowledge. Really knowing things is a different matter. You only know what you actually experience in your own life."

And now it is decided that education does mean that. Then who is best-educated man or woman in the town?

It is a question to be decided. Education then, as these men see

* This question is the crux of Anderson's great Winesburg story "The Untold Lie."

it, is knowledge. We here live at the edge of the country and the mountains. The best-educated person would be the one with the most actual knowledge of trees, wild life, fish in the streams, crops growing, domestic animals, soils in various parts of the county, the town, its history, the families here, the town government, some knowledge of general history, a knowledge of current history, got from reading intelligently, some knowledge of literature (It isn't the amount a man or woman reads. How much is understood of what is read?). Bible knowledge counts big, too.

Such a conversation may go on for a long time. A person of the town is fixed upon as the one, in the opinion of those present, having the best and most practical all-around education, the kind that best fits a person for intelligent living.

It would not do to reveal the person so chosen. It would, however, be interesting to get the opinion of the town, as a check on the decision of the town's conversational center.

And so the talk goes on, day after day, winter and summer. In late afternoon, Mr. Herbert goes home. "Lock the door when you go," he says, "and then turn out the lights."

The hour between five and six, particularly in the winter, is the best time for talk. Often the lights are not turned on. Men sit in half darkness, looking out into the street. Voices grow lower and the conversation takes a more serious turn. It is a masculine assembly, one of the few left.

Then, as the hour of six grows nearer, the men stumble out through the unlighted corridor of the courthouse into the street. No one takes too seriously the conversation in there. It is just talk. Very often it is mighty interesting talk though.

1930

A TRAVELER'S NOTES

April 3

In New Orleans . . . a gray day. It is cold. Yesterday a blizzard struck Chicago. Every time it is cold in Chicago, the tail of the blizzard-dog wags around down in this country.

The big flood of three years ago is still talked about by everyone down here. The city and all this country down here were in a tense state for weeks. Any day the water might have washed down on them, drowned them out.

In a flood the water does not break the levee down. It finds a weak place and seeps through. Then it begins to eat the levee away from beneath.

The city of New Orleans and all the country around are below the level of the river all the time. When the water rises to flood level, the ships sail up through the city with their decks at the level of the second and some third stories of houses.

There are water blisters in the streets and in gardens far from the river. There is a down-pressure of the water, a tremendous weight.

The ground is filled with water. In New Orleans great pumps are constantly pumping the water out of the ground.

There is a weak place in the earth's shell, let us say in your garden a half mile from the river.

Water begins to bubble up. It goes higher and higher. It becomes a fountain.

You have to plug it up, drive the water back down there.

The water is high this spring but not dangerously high. I crossed the river on the ferry and walked on the levee on the Algiers side.

There was a lonely stretch up-river, about a mile, and there I met a man. He was crazy. I thought of Marion and the insane people sometimes met on the streets there, men from the state hospital, harmless insane people who walk about.

This man made motions with his hands, as though signaling someone at a distance, far up-river. He stopped making queer motions with his hands and shouted strange words.

A look of terror and pain came over his face. He shouted louder and louder, made more violent motions and then suddenly grew quiet. He walked quietly enough past me, but when he had gone on for a hundred yards he went through it all again.

There was an old Negro cutting wood down at the river's edge and I went down the grassy slope of the levee to him. The floods bring drift logs down-river and deposit them on shore and the Negroes cut and saw them into firewood.

The old Negro told me that the man on the levee had been a railroad brakeman for twenty years. He and his brother were on the same freight-train crew. One day, in an absent-minded moment, he gave a wrong signal that got his brother killed.

So he went crazy brooding over it. Now he is on a pension from the railroad and walks all day, in all kinds of weather, on the levee by the river, trying to correct the mistake that caused his brother's death.

I spent Sunday far up-country on a strawberry farm. The farm has ten acres and it belongs to an Italian with a large family. They are growing rich on it.

The soil is very black and rich and the Italian raises strawberries for the fancy Northern market. He and his entire family work hard all year on the ten acres.

We walked about on the little farm. It was Sunday, March 23rd.

The little fields were clear and neat. Already they were shipping berries and the fields were all abloom. All the people in that neighborhood were Italians and they all raise strawberries. This week, and for sixty days now, they will be shipping many carloads by fast express every day.

There wasn't a weed on the entire farm. Between all the rows water had been piped in from a big artesian well. Every plant in the fields had had the personal attention of some member of the Italian family. The old grandmother had twelve long rows; the wife so many; the husband so many; each child so many. Each member of the family tried to out-do the others; each wanted to take me over his rows.

I had been in factory towns for weeks—people out of work, hungry, dissatisfied people standing about in the streets.

It was good to be with these people. They were simple, honest, kindly hard workers. They could laugh. In the factory towns you have little enough laughter, God knows.

We stayed in the field for two hours, where each plant among the thousands of plants had the personal attention of some member of the Italian's family, and then went into the house.

I'm a bit of a Wop myself. I like Italians.

The furnishings of the house were crude enough. It stood in the middle of the fields, an old, unpainted house. In there we all sat about a big table.

We ate bread and butter and drank wine made of strawberries. I had never tasted it before. It is very heavy and rich. The old Italian grandmother, who made me think of my own Italian grandmother,* made it.

We ate bread and drank and drank.

We talked about strawberry-raising. We talked of Italy.

We had more bread and more wine. I drank too much. It did not intoxicate me but it was too heavy and rich for me. On the way back to the city I was taken with a violent headache. I sat up in my bed all night, my head rocking with pain.

---

* Sherwood Anderson liked to pretend, against all evidence, that he was of Italian descent. His maternal grandmother, Margaret Austry, was actually born near Berlin, Germany.

A TRAVELER'S NOTES

May 22

From Marion to Grayson over the hills. The dogwood is in full bloom. I am a lucky man. I saw the dogwood come and go in the North Georgia hills and now I see the wonder again.

The rains are spotty this spring. You leave Marion in a shower. At the top of Iron Mountain the roads are dry. You pass through Troutdale. It is dry there. Two miles beyond, the roads are all become streams.

There is more ground being broken this spring than I have ever seen since coming to Virginia. There will be over-production. Things to eat will be cheap. We shall at least eat.

Money is of little use when things cost too much. As usual, because of the high tariffs, things the farmer has to buy will be dear and his own products will bring little.

The dry, late April and early May have held pastures back. Between Marion and Troutdale I picked up a farm woman with her two children. We spoke of the dry pasture. "Dry Mays make good crop years," she said.

In Grayson there are a number of widows. A good many men from there go out to the coal mines to work and often they do not come back. They are killed out there. It was so with the woman from whom I got my farm.

These women work hard. They are not afraid to go into the fields, hold the handle of a plow, hoe corn in season, cut corn, tend stock. Such a woman is left with a little poor mountain land and several children. She has fine courage. You seldom hear one of them whine. She buckles to, does a man's work, raises her kids, gives them what schooling she can.

Many country people are superstitious about killing cats. They declare it brings bad luck. We were burning brush on a hillside in the moonlight and a neighbor boy came, bringing a cat in a bag. The cat had been killing turkeys and chickens.

"Will you kill it?" he said to my son.

"Sure."

The cat was tied to a stake in the ground near a great brush fire. The moon shone down on him. My son raised his gun. Bang. That cat would kill no more young turkeys and chickens. We gave him the best send-off we could. We threw him in the roaring fire. Sparks flew far up into the clear, blue night sky. No doubt, this cat soon went flying on up with the sparks.

We should have had a dance on the hillside about the fire. If I could live again, I would choose to be born a savage. To the devil with all this modern business, automobiles, radios, factories, etc. Men and women singing and dancing in the moonlight for a poor dead cat. That would suit me.

There is a pink dogwood on the road from the printshop to the farm. It makes a vivid streak of color against a dark hill.

On the farm we get up early and go plunge in the creek. It is cold nowadays but it sure wakes a man up. In the evening we pitch horseshoes in an open grass plot by the creek. Neighbor men and boys come. We expect to develop some Grayson horseshoe pitchers who will make Smyth County look sick.

WATCH IT

August 21

This is going to be a grand year for a lot of people to get some education.

Tight times are ahead. Everyone has begun to realize that now, even the politicians. A lot of men, even here in our own county, who in ordinary years would be fairly prosperous farmers or workmen, are going to go broke this year. From being good, substantial, middle-class men, they are going to go plunk down into the working class.

It is going to be educational. We won't starve. We'll ride it through.

But we will find out some things.

We'll find out, for one thing, how helpless we are when we are the underdogs, how the game of life has been rigged against us—that is to say, the ordinary man.

Why, here we are. Here in this county there are beautiful export cattle that have to go to market, for which men paid ten to eleven cents a pound when they were feeders and that, after a year's feeding, will go at five cents.

See how much retail prices of meat are cut.

The country is perhaps drifting toward a crisis. We have a lot of men in politics who call themselves statesmen.

Watch and see what they have to offer.

Watch the rich and the successful. Nowadays clever men get rich on our general misfortunes. Watch and see if the rich draw in their horns any, if they strut any less, if they are any less the purse-proud.

A manufacturing company, for example, makes, let us say, in a flush year 30, 40, or even 50 or 100 percent on the money invested. Lots of them have done it recently. This year they will not make anything, or very little.

Watch and see if they distribute to the workers, to the men out of whose labor they have made all of this money, any of the profits out of the fat years behind.

Wait and see.

Will they try to help the workers now by the distribution of wealth made during the last five flush years or will they bellyache about hard times, no dividends, etc., and cut wages?

Wait and see.

This is sure going to be a very educational year for a lot of people.

OLD MISSISSIPPI RIVER MEN

December 25

There are a few old Mississippi River men left on the Mississippi. They are not all dead. A few packets still run out of New Orleans, Memphis, Vicksburg, Cairo, and St. Louis. Old river men still cling to them. Where one of them owns a packet or has been put in charge of her, he will have no one about him but old river men.

Other old captains who are also pilots will be in the pilothouse. There will be an old mate on deck. Old, decrepit river men get jobs as clerks or watchmen.

Captain Cooley of New Orleans is perhaps the oldest captain of a river packet on the river. He with his wife owns and lives on his own boat, never leaving her. She runs out of New Orleans up-river to Angola and then into the Red River. There is a state penal farm at Angola. She brings down staves, cut in the woods up there, that go to France and Spain to make wine barrels. She goes up loaded with sugar from the big sugar refineries in the lower river and in season brings down cotton for export. What a lot of sugar whiskey we drink nowadays.

The captain was a river man, owning his own packet in the river's flush days. He still owns his own boat. "I'll die on her," he says.

Uncle Henry Setler is a little old man of old river days who still is on the river. He has a job on a little packet boat that takes short trips out of one of the river towns and is often chartered for excursions. He is called the "bartender." What a comedown, really. Upstairs, in the little cabin, there is a stand where you may buy Coca Cola, chewing gum, cigarettes, cigars, and peanut candy. Uncle Henry keeps the stand and is paid five dollars a week.

Well, he gets his board; he gets a place to sleep. He told me, proudly, that since he has had this job, he has saved ninety-five dollars.

He is a very small man, past eighty now, but very much alive. Some years ago he had a stroke. For over a year he had to go about dragging one leg.

He didn't mind so much. To entertain other old river acquaintances who occasionally visited his boat, he used to take a pin out of his coat lapel and stick it deep into the leg. "See, it doesn't hurt at all," he said, smiling with childish pleasure.

One of the reasons that has made it possible for Uncle Henry to save his ninety-five dollars is that now he has no woman. For many years he was on a packet running out of Vicksburg. He has always been a man who does not smoke, drink, or gamble.

When he was in the Vicksburg trade he was clerk of a big boat and made good wages, but at the end of every trip he disappeared. When the boat was ready to sail again he reappeared with a blackened eye and perhaps with bruised lips. Someone had been beating him.

It was for a long time a mystery to the other river men. One night, however, the boat arrived at Vicksburg late, and there was a child, a little girl of six, waiting to greet Henry. When the boat landed and he went ashore, she hurried toward him. He caught her quickly up in his arms and ran up the bank but the pilot of the boat, filled with curiosity, turned a searchlight on the pair.

It was a colored child.

"Well, then, she is my daughter," Uncle Henry explained later. She was the illegitimate child of a huge old colored woman of Vicksburg.

Afterward the big colored woman got bold and, when she was drunk, would sometimes come to the boat and demand money from Henry. If he refused, she beat him. The river men stuck to Henry. "He's one of us. It is bum luck, his falling for such a woman," they said.

Then the child died and he got out of her clutches.

Uncle Henry loves to tell of the good times when he was young and a big man. He declares he was once prosperous. He owned a boat of his own on the Sunflower River, a tiny packet called "The Grand Turk," and in some of the towns along the river he owned a livery stable.

There was a woman of one of the towns along the river who took money from men. Henry always recommended her highly. She paid him a commission.

"You see," he says, "I was a big man. I owned a steamboat, a livery stable, two hacks, and a woman. They all made money for me. You should have seen how the money rolled in."

He declares that ill luck came his way because once, in an evil day, he took as passengers on "The Grand Turk" at the same time a white mule, a red-haired woman, and a preacher.

The boat sank. It struck a snag and sank. All on board except only Uncle Henry were drowned. This was in a deeply wooded place. It was night. How Uncle Henry escaped he doesn't know. In some miraculous way, however, he crept ashore.

"I was lost in the deep woods for three days," he says. When at last he made his way out of the woods his livery stable had burned with all his horses, hacks, etc.

"But what of the woman, Uncle Henry?"

"She died of grief. She had heard I was drowned."

Captain Tom Smith is a pilot on one of the few packets still running. I knew him when I used to be about down here five or six years ago. He is a solidly built old man with a red face, white hair, and false teeth. His teeth do not fit very well.

Once, when I was on a trip with him, he had got a preparation at a drugstore to make his teeth stay in his mouth. It was some kind of glue. He pasted them in. They got stuck in so fast he couldn't get them out at all. He told me that. "My mouth is terribly sore," he said. "I can't eat. I can't sleep."

At last, fortunately, the preparation dissolved.

I had given Captain Tom a copy of a novel of mine called *Poor White*. He read it and the mate of the boat read it.

It was read by the engineer of a river tug. The three men were great cronies and when they were not on the river used to sit together in a little place in New Orleans. One day they sent for me.

It was Captain Tom who did the talking.

"Now you look here," he said, "in this book you gave me you have got a certain man. His name is Hugh.

"So he is about to get married.

"He is upstairs in a house. His bride is in another room.

"She is in the bedroom.

"It is his marriage night.

"So he does not go to her. Suddenly he takes off his shoes. He puts up a window and climbs out onto a roof.

"He crawls down the roof and leaps to the ground. He runs away.

"Why did he do that?

"Is it to decide a bet?

"Is it to settle an argument?"

"He did it for this reason—well, you see, he had married the woman. He did not feel she respected him really, as a man, I mean.

"Women marry men sometimes they do not respect. He thought she had done that."

"I see. And so he ran away."

"Yes, he ran away."

"I said so," declared Captain Tom. "That was my argument. That was what I said. I argued that all along."

There are a good many small river packets that belong now to the government. They are used to take men who do levee work up and down the river. Some of them are fitted up quite sumptuously. Generals who are engineers ride on them. Sometimes the generals have guests. Men and women who are in society come to visit these boats. Other army officials come. Sometimes men who are in Congress—senators and the like—ride on the river.

There is an old river man, a pilot named Captain Sam, who works on such a boat. He is a huge old man with a red face and chews tobacco incessantly. He is famous for his profanity. Like all old river men he has contempt for army engineers. More than once I have talked this matter over with him. They are always, he declares, telling what they are going to do to the river.

They are going to control it. They will straighten the channel. They will build spillways. They will make the Mississippi behave itself.

Captain Sam, like all old river men, does not think the engineers have enough reverence for the Mississippi. He thinks they are upstarts. All old river men are in their hearts pagans. They are Mississippi worshipers. When engineers talk, as they sometimes do, with a great deal of assurance, these old river men say nothing. In secret they spit, swear, and shake their heads. It is to them as though some man had spoken too lightly of God.

There was an engineer, a general, on his boat—a sumptuously furnished boat with comfortable beds, a good cook and all—and he had guests.

There came two United States senators with their secretaries and two congressmen with their ladies.

The general was in uniform. There were other army officers on board in uniforms.

All of them were standing on the lower deck of the boat—on the prow. On these sternwheel river packets the lower deck is within a foot or two of the water.

It was late afternoon, and the packet—with all these precious passengers aboard standing there enjoying the view—the packet was making its way rather slowly upstream.

It was at the time of high water. The packet was going toward a distant city. The general with his distinguished guests was to get off there; they were to dine there.

The packet, to avoid the weight of the current, was creeping along slowly close inshore.

What the general and his guests did not know was that there was a cut-off just there.

A cut-off is a shallow strip of water across a narrow neck of land where the river makes a great loop. You can run a cut-off in high water, but when the river goes down you have to go around. All the river men like to tell how General Grant, with many army engineers and thousands of men, spent a whole winter trying to enlarge a cut-off to get around the city of Vicksburg during the Civil War.

They wanted to leave Vicksburg away back in the country, away from the river. They wanted to turn the river itself through the cut-off.

But the river wouldn't behave. It wouldn't do it.

Years afterward, when Grant and his engineers were gone, the river itself suddenly one day made up its own mind to go through that cut-off. It did it, too. They never did get Vicksburg back on the river proper. They had to dig a canal to it.

So there was Captain Sam piloting that boat that day and there were all those important figures on the lower deck, on the prow, and there was a cut-off just there. The guests did not know about the cut-off but Captain Sam did. He knew there was water enough to get through.

It was almost impossible to see the entrance to the cut-off. The entrance was concealed by tall, fast-growing willow trees.

And so the guests did not understand what was up that day when Captain Sam, at the wheel of that packet, suddenly turned her nose inshore and whistled down the tube for more steam. They just stood there asking one another questions. One of the senators was asking the other if he had ever read *Huckleberry Finn.* They were, you see, having a literary conversation.

And then the boat dashed into the willows. It went smash through them. There were a lot of Negro deck hands, waiters, etc., standing about on the aft part of the boat. They were inconsiderate enough to whoop and shout with delight.

You see, the general, the big engineer, in his fine uniform, got knocked off into the river—it wasn't deep; he didn't drown—he just got all covered with muddy water. He could grab a willow and get ashore—he could have leaped ashore.

But all the others had to fall to their hands and knees and crawl. The branches of the willows were raking the low decks. They had to crawl toward the Negroes standing aft in the boat and laughing at them.

Captain Sam saved nearly two hours going through that cut-off. He always swore he didn't know there was anyone on deck. You know where the pilothouse is on a river packet, perched away up on top of the boat. You can't see the lower deck from up there.

Captain Sam lost his job for doing what he did that day, endangering the lives of all those distinguished people, but he didn't care. Some other old river captain, on some of the old packets that still run up and down the river, gave him a job at once. There were quite a few old pilots on the river who would have given up their own jobs rather than see Captain Sam out of a berth after that.

1931

AN ANSWER

February 26

There is a curious notion abroad. It is, I am sure, partly defensive. Some time ago I gave out to a representative of the Associated Press an interview speaking rather cheerfully of the possibilities of country editorship as a way of life. In the interview I did not hold up the job of country editorship as a way to enter the golden gates without a pass. There are a lot of corking good country editors now. Also there are a lot of bright young men and women looking for a way of life that will give them a bit more satisfaction in the end than becoming cogs in the city newspaper game or going into business. Particularly in the South there are a good many of these young men and women who have a prejudice against the business life. Most of them become young lawyers now. Already in the South there are about four times as many lawyers as the South needs or can conveniently use. There are some corking good country editors but there are a lot more not so corking. A lot of the exchanges that come to our desk, Isabel,* are as dull as dish water.

But I did not sit down to speak of that. I really wanted to call your hand a bit about the excitement, the adventure, the danger, etc., of most city newspaper work. Isn't that a bit overdone? I am addressing you in particular among a lot of comments and letters received because you are a woman, and I think the opportunities for a good deal of fun out of life in country journalism are as great for women as for men. When you speak, Isabel, of all the excitement in city newspaper work, aren't you rather overdoing the matter? Aren't you a bit on the defensive?

The drift of American life now, for the last several generations, has sent most of our brighter young men and women to the cities. I do not deny that. I would like to help start a little counter-drift if I could. I would like to be a little worm in the fair apple of progress. I would like to steer some of the brighter youngsters like yourself, for example, back toward the towns.

There is no question, Isabel, but that the cityward drift has robbed the towns. Life in the towns does tend toward a kind of sameness. There is a tremendous fear of new ideas. What has come to the towns from the cities and what is coming hasn't helped much.

Still it seems to me that intellectual dullness—want of color and variety to life—is hardly a peculiarity of the smaller towns. The notion abroad that life in the larger cities does not grow dull, that there is something specially to be gained by living always in the midst of herds of people, does not at least check with my own experience. What is coming to the towns now from the cities isn't so high-class.

For example, there is the radio.

It is pretty much supported by business, by advertising. Think of what it might be and then think of what, on the whole, it is.

* Isabel Foster, in an editorial published in the *Hartford* (Connecticut) *Courant*, had written in response to an Associated Press interview with Anderson about his newspapers: "Quite frankly the novelist is going to tell young men and women that, while they cannot expect to make much money, their rewards will be comparable to those of the country doctor and the country lawyer. He does not make clear, however, that he is going to warn them of isolation from all others of their temperament, of the dullness of days of detail. He seems also to be leaving out of consideration the typical young newspaper writer's thirst for superlatives, for excitement, even for danger, though he must know that too much routine lays waste the powers of such spirits so that wonder goes out of life and cynicism takes its place." Anderson reprinted Isabel Foster's remarks with his reply.

Advertisements of goods being bawled into millions of homes day and night, wise-crackers always cracking at us, the clever little smart-alecks among city men always shouting at us.

There are things enough to be said against life in the average American town right now. City snobbishness has come. There is the same fear of ideas you will find in the city. We people of the towns see each other pretty closely and pretty constantly. None of us will bear seeing very often. We are not, to any great extent, very much interested in making life more cheerful or more wholesome for each other.

There is, however, a lot on the other side of the ledger.

There is nature, for example. Don't smile, please. There are the hills and the streams and the forests, always to the small-town man close at hand. Man, any man of sensibilities, living in the world now, needs nature as perhaps man never needed it before. He needs religion, real religion, the nameless sort of silent thing that comes as he stands in forest paths, a feeling of life outside man, in trees, in animals, the earth itself, even, if you will, in insects.

Industrialism—the modern madness for wealth at any price, the domination of so much of life by money, the nerve tensions due to speed madness, goods madness—surely needs something to counter-act it.

I think there is a better chance to get this thing in the towns than there is in the cities. For myself, I can say that, since I have been spending so many of my days these last few years in a small town, I have been able to do reading I have been wanting to do for years.

It is true there are certain things I miss. I have, for example, rather a passion for painting and I do not see much here.

I do, however, see the changing colors in our hills. Please do not at once accuse me of sentimentality, Isabel. I see the bare lines of the hills in winter, the subtle, changing winter colors, the spring colors, the fall colors. There is a lot of sky down where I am. I see the changing seasons, horses pulling plows across fields, the fields being painted with rather delicate, changing colors thus.

I do occasionally, Isabel, go to sit alone in some wood. I can get to a dozen such places in my cheap car in five minutes where I sit silently. Is this dullness; is this sameness? I even pray a bit some-times—my own kind of prayer.

For myself, I have no feeling of any very direct or personal relationship with what men call God. He doesn't owe me anything. Life doesn't owe me much. I don't know what God is, what he wants of me, if he wants anything. I am not going to take any man's word on this matter.

There are, however, certain feelings that occasionally sweep over me when I am alone thus, no other man or woman about, no one in sight. It can compensate me for missing a lot of what you speak of as the excitement, danger, adventure, etc., of present-day city life. It compensates for a lot of loneliness that even books cannot take away.

Is all of this necessarily just an older man's feeling? I seem to remember having just such feeling when I was young. Life is a queer tangle, God knows. I cannot comprehend it. Can you?

I have, however, a notion that there is a rather tremendous opportunity in country journalism for a lot of people of all ages, rather like me, just as we are, I am pretty sure, coming into a time of a wider, deeper questioning of many things in American life than we have ever known. I think it is going to be a healthy time. The churches are going to be questioned, the politicians, the educators. In literature I look for the end of the day of the wise-crackers and the smart-alecks. Why, I think people will even dare to be serious without feeling too apologetic about it. There might even be more laughter. Success itself—the great American myth of the glory of bigness, of owning more land than you can farm, having more money than you can spend, making a louder noise in the world than another—even all this may be questioned.

To expect happiness from tackling such a job as being editor of an obscure country paper in an obscure country town is absurd. To expect happiness anywhere as any very prolonged state of being is absurd.

I think the job is an interesting one. I think it is a good job for the brightest young men and women in the country. In the interview given the Associated Press, I was really trying to say just that and no more. If you, Isabel, think that I, a man of the varied experiences in life you speak of, if you think that I expect to achieve happiness either in a small town or in a city, you give me credit for being more naïve than I am.

MORE TRAVEL NOTES

March 19

A side street in a Southern industrial city, on a Saturday afternoon. Thoughts. This is in Georgia. There is a muddy, yellow river flowing by the city and in the distance can be seen the red hills and roads of Georgia.

The red fields and the roads are streaked with yellow. There is much abandoned land. Pines make a clean forest and few other trees grow down here. There is a peculiarity about pine trees. The trees at the heart of the forest throw off few seeds while those at the outer rim scatter them far and wide. The forests all have clean floors, carpeted with brown pine needles. Young slash pine are growing everywhere. A scientist tells me that these young pine contain little resin and are therefore available for paper-making. He is working away at the problem of utilizing the millions of acres of abandoned Southern farm lands by reforesting. The hot sun helps. It will make young pine available for paper-making in fifteen years, while, he says, it takes sixty years to develop the Canadian spruce now being used.

A man who knows tells me of the peculiar poverty of so much of Southern agriculture. The land, he says, has been cotton-cropped to death. The county agents and the state agricultural departments preach diversified farming to build up the land but nothing can be raised without the use of commercial fertilizers. When the farmer goes to the bank in town to borrow money for fertilizer and seed, he can get none unless he agrees to plant only cotton.

That is because cotton cannot be eaten by the farmer's family or by the poor livestock he may own. Often cotton is planted right up to the farmhouse door. The whole system of agriculture in the

South is bad. No doubt it grew out of the old plantation system. After the Civil War the Southern landowner had nothing but his land. He began letting it out in small pieces to poor white farmers and to the blacks. Tiny little tenant houses were built. In a stretch of country like our own Rich Valley there will be ten times as many houses and families as are in the Rich Valley. The raising of cotton takes a great deal of work. From the time the ground is prepared in the spring and until the crop is harvested, beginning, say, in October, the crop must be worked some fourteen times. A whole poor family will be at work all summer on twenty acres of land. The crop must also be chopped out—that is to say, thinned out; it must be picked by hand, a slow, laborious job. The whole plot of ground, right up to the tenant house door, is set out to cotton. There is often no garden at all.

The houses are poor, miserable sheds and the people are very, very poor. Within a day's journey of Atlanta, Georgia, there are hundreds of thousands of people whose whole income amounts to less than eighty dollars a year.

How do they live on such an amount? The answer is that they do not live. They merely exist. They are ignorant and undernourished. Pellagra, a disease due to undernourishment, flourishes.

In the South you get, more than in any other part of America, the sharp distinction between wealth and poverty. Modern industry has brought wealth to many of the cities. The cotton mills, started often through desperation in order to furnish some kind of work to the poor, half-starved whites, have prospered.

They have been able to maintain low wages and thus get the best of Northern competition because of the vast supply of poor labor always available. Any kind of wages seems large to people accustomed to an income of eighty dollars a year. The cotton mill owners claim to have been a real benefit to the people in bringing them into the towns, housing them in decent houses, providing schooling, etc., and there is a lot to be said for the claim.

But they have got rich. How many rich men excuse everything by saying, "I give people work"!

You would think that was all they thought about. As a matter of fact, they have got rich on the labor of these poor people.

They are brought in off the plains and off the hills. In the South, among the poor, you do not think of the wages of a man as supporting a wife and family as you do, so often, in the North. On the farms the wife and children work in the fields and, when they go to town to live in a cotton mill village, the entire family goes to work in the mill.

There are cruel enough parents, too—"mill daddies," so called. These are men who go to town to put the wife and children to work in the mill while they do nothing. They live on the wages of the wife and the children.

There are laws in some of the states regulating the age at which a child may go to work in a mill, but there are none on the farms. The child in the mill village often has two ages—the real age and the mill age.

In the towns the poor people, herded off by themselves in the mill villages, do not become a part of the life of the town. They do not sink into the town life and become citizens. Often the mill and the mill village are just outside the corporation limit. There is enough cruelty among poor people, too. You have heard of the untouchables of India. Of course, the employees of the mill villages, the "lint heads," are not like that, but there is a suggestion of it. The poor workman in town is anxious to feel himself above someone; so he takes it out on the mill hand. He treats the mill hand with scorn and the mill hand retaliates by hating the town man. Often the mill owners are ten times as charitable as the poor people, the merchants, lawyers, etc., of the towns. Human nature isn't so nice. Mark Twain said that the more he saw of people the more he liked dogs.

In town, in a Southern industrial town, on Saturday afternoon. It is early March but flowers are beginning to appear. There has been a warm rain. Great piles of oranges and grapefruit are piled before the stores. The mill hands are having a half-day off and go in groups through the street. Farmers arrive in town in broken-down wagons, drawn by bony mules.

It is a place of color and of life.

There is a street of Negroes. They gather everywhere along the sidewalks. Phonographs are going. The Negroes, for some peculiar reason, stand the hardship of life down here better than the whites. They do not worry. The long, hot summers do not make them white and thin. They laugh. The men and women flirt and play on the sidewalks. It is hard to keep away from them. They seem the center of what happiness, what satisfaction in life is to be found now in the Southern scene.

H O R N I E S : Late March Days

April 9

I am getting as bad as Tom Rider and Emmett Sprinkle. Presently, like Tom I shall chuck all work and go fishing every day. I shall never, however, be an expert like Burt Dickinson.

I began thinking of hornies driving up from the South. When they bite well they bite with a quick viciousness that is exciting. They are great bait-eaters. You have to be quick.

On the river bank below Red Bridge. There was a young girl fishing there. I sat down near her. I thought she could not be more than fourteen but she said she was eighteen. She began telling me of her operations. She was operated on at a Roanoke hospital and had three doctors. She was proud of that.

Her father came and fished with us and then a young man came. He said his father worked at the Lincoln but that he stayed at home and did some farming. We all fished. No luck.

There were gray clouds drifting across the sky. Conversation as to the moods of the fishes. "When the wind is in the south it blows the hook in the fish's mouth," etc. The wind was in the east.

Driving out to that place, I had seen a young wheat field on a hill. The wheat had been drilled in. The ground on the hill was bright yellow. The young wheat was not yet high enough to hide the yellow ground underneath.

The yellow shone through the young green, giving a new vividness to it. In some places the ground underneath was red. The whole field was alive.

At the river a young man, Jack Buchanan, from over near the Red Bridge, came down in a car. There was a ford there but he missed it and the water flowed up over the engine. He had a girl in the car with him.

He crawled out on the running board of the car and shouted. I shouted at him, offering him a fish pole. "You might as well fish," I said. "You're stuck." He had on an overcoat and, as he crawled about on the running board of his car, the tails of the coat were in the stream.

A young man came from plowing in a nearby field and pulled him out. "There is that fellow fishing down there," he said to the farm boy. "I bet he'll put this in the paper." He drove off. The farm boy came and told me.

I went to another place where there were several young men fishing. I saw a series of newly plowed fields all on hillsides, the color of the soil changing a dozen times in one field. All the colors kept changing in the light.

I stopped on a bridge. I had a letter in my pocket from a friend. That was a good place to read it. He had been walking and had stopped by a bridge. He looked over and saw the yellow bottom of the stream from above. He wanted to paint that. I remembered a dry creek bed seen once farther south. That was in a clay country. There were hills of blue clay, yellow clay, and red clay. Rains had washed clay of various colors down into the creek bed and the dry bottom was all awash with color.

My friend said Monet once painted water lilies as seen in a stream from a bridge.

At the new place the fish bit better but the stream was swift and I did not have enough sinkers on my line. A young farmer had to go home to do his chores and so gave me the sinker off his line. The fish would not bite for me.

A boy came, a tough little boy. He kept swearing as he fished but he caught fish. Another illusion destroyed. He said he did not go to school. "They can't make me go," he said. "Why not?" I asked.

Another boy came, this one with yellow hair and blue eyes. The tough boy began to brag about North Carolina, where he lived. He said the girls were sure tough down there. He spoke to the yellow-haired boy. "If you tried to go to school there do you know what the girls would do to you?"

"No."

"They'd tear your pants off."

"Not mine. I bet they wouldn't."

"They would, too."

"They wouldn't neither."

"They would."

The controversy went on and on. "They would." "They wouldn't." The tough little boy took a chew of tobacco, swore, and went away. I had caught no hornies; so he sold me what he had. I wanted to make a showing in town. The yellow-haired boy said the tough boy had charged me too much. "He stuck you," he said. It was beginning to get dark. There were more newly plowed fields near and they were nice. My friend's letter had quoted a line of poetry that kept running through my head: "This wary winter that was white so long."

"The North Carolina girls wouldn't tear my pants off," the yellow-haired boy said quietly. His blue eyes were serious about it. He said he thought the tough little boy was only talking big. "Why should they want to tear my clothes off?" he asked.

I told him I had been in North Carolina and had got through all right. No one had touched my clothes, I said, and the statement seemed to bring great relief to his mind.

A TRAVELER'S NOTES

April 23

In a North Carolina cotton mill town. It lies on a great plain with hills seen in the distance. Often I leave home and come to a town like this.

I go to a hotel, not the first one but the one just a bit off first-class.

Some of the people of the town live there. At the newest hotel there is likely too much stir and bustle for me.

"I may be here several days. Make me a good rate. Put me up high as you can." I go to look at the room.

"This one will not do. Show me another, and another."

I am particular about the view. I like to look out over the land. A corner room is best.

I have registered as S. Anderson. There are hotel clerks who are sometimes literary. It seems unbelievable, but it is true.

Then there are young writers, like the two Bob's on this paper, who, wanting news, go look at hotel registers sometimes. They would come and interview a man.

"What do you think of Mr. Dreiser slapping Mr. Lewis?" *

"Who do you think is the greatest living poet?"

Bah. I do not want to be interviewed. At present I am in a very delicate situation. I have got into a certain story I have been writing, a certain woman.

She is tall, a rather snake-like creature who will not behave. She keeps doing and saying things that, if I am not careful, will destroy my story.

Or make it something I never had in mind.

For the time, I do not want to see anyone, do not want to talk—least of all about writing. I do not want any letters.

There will be letters from some publisher, an editor. "Where is that book you promised? Can you do us an article about so and so?"

"No.

"Damn your bleary eyes. Let me alone."

It is nice to be in among people just living their lives. When you are not in your room at work you wander about.

There is a ball game, two high school teams playing in a little park. You go sit on a bench beside a man. A conversation begins.

"Do you live here?"

"No, I am just traveling."

"What do you sell?"

* At a party in New York, on March 19, 1931, Sinclair Lewis and Theodore Dreiser quarreled and Dreiser slapped Lewis three times, while Lewis each time "turned the other cheek."

Here is my opportunity. I make up lies.

"I sell carpets."

Or carpet sweepers, or billiard balls, or railroad ties.

The man to whom you are talking is curious about you. It doesn't last long. He begins to tell you about himself. There is his main interest.

He is a man who almost got rich once. He speculated in real estate. There was one time when, if he had sold out, cleaned up, he would have had a hundred thousand dollars.

He was a fool and didn't do it. Now he is broke.

He is quite cheerful about it. "Are you interested in baseball?" He is. He tells you about it. He has read a book by one George Herman Ruth, commonly known as "Babe."

"You have heard about him?"

"Sure. Who hasn't?"

He explains the difference between these high school boys playing ball and the professionals.

The professionals, he says, study the business—he calls it "a business"—they think about it all the time.

"Like writers, professionals—the difference between them and the amateurs, eh?

"The ones who hope vaguely they will be writers someday, but who read nothing, do not know literature." This is something you think. You do not say it.

The man on the bench tells you what Babe Ruth said in his book. There were certain young pitchers. They had curves, speed, everything. They called Ruth over to watch them work.

"Tell me how I am. How am I?" they ask.

"Well, if I were you, I'd spend about two years learning to get the ball over the plate."

Little touches coming to a man. Hide yourself, be quiet, look at life.

The maid comes to make the room. She is a great, strapping black woman with a wide mouth and a body many white women would give a good deal to have.

You get into conversation with her. Her name is May. She had a man once but he died.

He was a good man. When payday came what he got in his pay envelope was just what he brought home. He left two kids on her.

She is a big, strong, brown woman, only twenty-eight, and admits at once that she would like to get another man.

They aren't so easy to get, not the right sort. There are a lot of big, strong colored men, she says, who only want a woman to work for them.

They are always beating a woman or knocking her about.

On the other hand, she says, a woman does want a man. When she has once had one it's hard to do without. She hasn't given up. She is still looking about.

The trouble is that what good ones there are, some other woman already has.

"Would you take a good one from another woman?"

"Yes, sir, I guess, if I could, and I had the chance."

Such a woman works in the hotel from seven in the morning until five in the afternoon. She gets ten dollars a week. Traveling men don't give chamber maids many tips. She is always making beds for white men she never sees.

There aren't many men come who sit around in their rooms for hours, writing or walking up and down, as I do.

Old women are the worse, she says; they are so fussy.

She thinks that women, when they get older, when they have lost interest, when they don't care much whether they stay in with men or not, do surely get hard to get along with.

She hopes she doesn't ever get like that. After all, she is only twenty-eight. She may yet get her another good man.

She would take a chance, quicker than she does, only she is afraid he might not be good to her kids.

TRAVEL NOTES: Speakeasy

June 11

There is a certain shocking trait in Anglo-Saxon people that those of us who are Americans without being very Anglo-Saxon will never understand. It is the trait of being satisfied with a blind statement made and being at the same time quite blind to facts. The writer has been traveling about a good deal lately. He has been to several large cities and to colleges and universities. He has been to coal-mining towns where he has seen people living in physical conditions that are shocking. As he has traveled about he has, of course, read the daily papers. In the dailies he reads constantly statements from big industrialists. "Everything is all right," they keep saying. A banker says it. Next day a man who manufactures locomotive engines says it. "We are turning the corner. The corner has been turned, etc."

Recently I went for a two-day walk through the great industrial sections of the towns of Newark and Jersey City. It was like walking over a battlefield after a great battle. There are silent factories everywhere. Here is a small factory running on half-time and beside it, on both sides, are great structures dead and silent. Boys have come creeping up to break the windows in the factories. They always do that. The poet Lindsay once wrote a poem called "Why do boys always break factory windows?" * It is a question worth asking. Is there feeling growing at last in people, deep down in people, that the whole American scheme of putting no stop at all to what is called individual enterprise, to putting into the hands of individuals this terrific new thing in the world called the machine, letting each man who can get control do what he pleases with it,

* Anderson was thinking of the title and first line of Vachel Lindsay's "Factory Windows Are Always Broken."

letting one industry destroy another, creating a waste constantly in what is presumed to be peaceful times that is worse than war waste, the automobile now destroying the railroads, presently the airplane destroying the automobile—is there really a question growing in people's minds? It would be nice to know.

Mr. Jim Farrell makes a speech to brother steel men in New York. Mr. Charley Schwab has just got through talking. Charley has been very cheerful, a booster. "Everything is O.K.," he cries. He thinks the steel men have been very noble in the way in which they have maintained wages, for example. He sits down smiling and then Jim gets up. Jim was once a steelworker himself. He says that all Charley has been saying is pure bunk. Wages are not being maintained. Men are in most factories working at best two or three days a week. And the wages for those few days' work are being cut. Ten percent this month and another ten percent next month. Jim says he also has been down into the coal-mining towns. "We ought to be ashamed of the way in which great masses of American people are living," he says. Evidently, he said too much. They shut him up, apparently. The next day he got over it. He began to crawfish. He began giving out interviews saying everything was, after all, O.K. What happened to Jim? I guess he forgot that this is a speakeasy country. You don't tell what you see. You shut your eyes. That's the way. Are we to believe Jim while he is speaking out or while he is later crawfishing out of it?

What about prohibition? I went to New York. I saw men there go into stores and buy liquor—into stores, mind you, where they were as unknown as I was and buy liquor as freely as I would go into Frank Copenhaver's store in Marion and buy a dozen grapefruit. I saw this. A man went and did it to show me. It can be done, I'm told, as freely as that in thousands of stores in New York, Chicago, Philadelphia, and a dozen other cities. I have never been in a hotel in America where the bellhop who takes you to your room is not ready to get you all the liquor you want in three minutes.

In New York you dine in speakeasies. There is some little faint bluff at concealment. The speakeasies are in basements along almost every street in the town. You go in through a basement door.

Automobiles are parked everywhere along the street. The places are all right. The food is good. They do not cost more than other eating places. Usually there is a bar. Women and girls come in and stand with the men at the bars. It's all right with me if people like it that way. I never did believe you could change people much by passing laws. If people want to make drinking seem smart and a bit strange and mysterious it's O.K., I guess.

But I do get fed up on this whole speakeasy tone to all of life. It makes me tired.

For example, there is Russia. Obviously few of us know much about what they are doing and how it will come out. On the face of it there is apparently an effort being made to give life a new tone, not a speakeasy tone. As I understand it, they are trying to turn the machine, that has been such a gloriously adventurous thing with us and that is now so evidently dangerously out of hand, they are trying—it is said—to make the machine work for all instead of the few. They have got a plan. They are working on the plan.

Where is our plan? What are we doing about it?

What are our politicians doing? We are in a curious state as regards industry, farming, prohibition, merchandising. A good many men you meet nowadays do think we have turned a corner . . . not the corner the so-called "statesmen" are always talking about but another corner. A good many men think nowadays that all of modern civilization is at pause. There is a strange listlessness. Men tell me it has invaded what factories are still running and that it is in every office. In many places men are no longer interested in their work. "What's the use?" they say. "If we get over this depression we'll just run into another in a few years," they say. The modern, highly mechanized factories seem to take all the life and spirit out of workmen in a few years. "What about our children? Are they going to be up against the same racket we are up against? Is life just a racket? Is it just a cheap game?"

Men everywhere ask that question and then stand with their hands at their side. "The best thing to do is to go get drunk," a man said to me, only last week.

"There isn't going to be anything done. No one has any plan. If anyone here had a plan, he wouldn't say anything.

"This is a speakeasy country," he said.

Has it come in the end to that? Was the man right? Are we to go on always facing times like this with no plan that has anything to do with modern industrial life? Are we, alas, truly a speakeasy country?

LAZY NEWSPAPERS

August 13

There are plenty of that kind. Most men are lazy. They are not necessarily physically lazy. They are mentally lazy. A profound mental laziness has become characteristic of America. Our women are better. Many of them at least try to lift themselves out of the morass of dead words, dead thoughts, empty phrases by which most of us live.

There was never such a people to live by phrases. Say a thing often enough and everyone will apparently believe. There is such an expression, let's say, as "Southern hospitality." Surely the South is hospitable, that is to say, certain people of the South are hospitable. There are enough that are not. I have lived in the East, in the Middle West, in the far West, and in the South. I can't see any difference as regards hospitality. A few weeks ago I was driving toward a certain Southern town. There was a big signboard at the edge of town. "If you want to know true Southern hospitality go to the Central Hotel."

Hospitality at a hotel indeed! There is a glad-hander waiting for you at the door. The clerk is sizing you up. How much can he soak you for a room? Hospitality, as I understand it, is a free thing freely given. It isn't commercialized. But we have commercialized everything, even Southern hospitality. You see what phrases come to. They are picked up and made into advertising slogans.

But I started to speak of newspapers, the laziness of newspapers.

I would like to say something about the dailies and about the country weeklies.

Our country weeklies in America might be something. Some of them are. At least they are trying to be.

But first let me speak of the dailies. You should go some day, when you have the opportunity, into the editorial rooms of a big daily. Here is a newspaper of sixteen, twenty-four, even sixty-five pages. How much of it do you think is prepared in the newspaper office itself? Mighty little of it.

An amazingly large proportion of it is canned stuff. It may be that is necessary if such a large paper is to be printed. To fill such a paper with anything like live stuff would take an army of people. Every section, even of a large city, would have to be thoroughly covered. Certainly that isn't done.

What happens is that there are, nowadays, in every big newspaper office, certain telegraphic machines. News, opinions, statements, the records of sporting events—these all come into the office of the newspaper over the wire. There is an electrically run machine that types the stuff as it comes in. It rolls out of the machines all typed, ready to go to the printer. What happens is that the editor sits there running his eyes over the strips. Most of the work in newspaper offices nowadays is done with a pair of scissors. You throw in a little local stuff, what you can get hurriedly, and then depend upon the automatic machine for the rest.

As I say, these things may be necessary if you are to run a big modern daily. I do not know. I know this. Buy an American newspaper in a city of Louisiana, in Maine, in California, and they are all pretty much alike, pretty much in the same tone. They have really become big commercial ventures. Businessmen own and run most of them. That is the reason they are always on the side of big business. They are, as a rule, as subservient to big business as is the modern so-called "statesman."

Big business also controls the movies; it controls the radio.

There is a peculiarity of American life that you have perhaps not thought about. In America few people buy anything at all. Everything is sold to people.

For example, there is the modern popular magazine. It is owned and run by a businessman. Naturally, his big problem is circulation. The magazine, being run as a business enterprise, must think first of all of the advertisers. What do the advertisers want? That is the big, the primary question.

Suppose we in this little newspaper office here wanted to expand one of our sheets into a national weekly or monthly. The immediate problem would be to get circulation.

There are all sorts of schemes worked to get circulation. One of the favorite ones is to send out, during the summer, a bunch of rather good-looking young men and women. Such a young businessman comes to your door: "I am working my way through college." There is little enough said about the magazine he is selling you; very likely, the least said the better.

You can get a certain kind of cheap magazine, very well put up, for three years by paying only fifty cents. The money paid for subscriptions to any magazine or newspaper of large circulation doesn't pay the cost of printing it. What pays is the resultant increase in advertising. Do you wonder big business controls public opinion?

When we took over these two small newspapers here in Smyth County, there was a good deal of interest taken in the enterprise. It may be the writer is at fault. He likes small-town and country life, the intimacy of it, the people met, the nearness to the fields, the hills, and the forests.

As a matter of fact, I have written a good deal about small-town life. I think the possibilities of such a life might be increased by small-town and county local weeklies, run by men or women interested in their work. I have written about that. I have spoken about it to students in colleges. I have even tried to interest certain rich men, trying to get them to establish a fund so that money may be loaned to the right kind of young men and women who want to go into such work.

But a country newspaper can be utterly lazy and no-account, too. The truth is that most of them are. When I had written some articles setting forth, as best I could, the possibilities in this work and had spoken on the subject at several colleges, I began to be besieged with letters. They began to pour in.

Now it is my notion about a country weekly that it is not just an organ for one man, to express one man's opinion. I think a country editor should have his say but he should give others a chance to have their say, too. No country newspaper is exactly private property. It usually isn't forced on people as are the large magazines and weeklies. For example, almost all of the subscribers to our Smyth County papers come into the printshop here and subscribe voluntarily. It is true that just now one of our editors is making a tour of the county. He aims before he is through to visit every house in Smyth County. Naturally, he is taking subscriptions as he goes but he isn't telling anyone that he is doing it to pay his way through college or any such nonsense. He is doing it primarily to get acquainted. After all, we have only been running these papers three or four years. We want to know everyone in the county personally, if that is possible, how our readers live, where they live, what they are like.

We do not believe that the country weekly should be in competition with the dailies. For that matter, we wish there could be a few dailies as free and unhampered as the rightly-run country weekly can be, but that is not our problem. We believe that life here, in an American country town and in the country about, can be as dignified, as interesting, as worthwhile as any life. There isn't anyone going to score us off by calling us a "hick." We have met too many New York hicks, Chicago hicks, Paris and London hicks. Life is, after all, largely a matter of human relationships. This writer has, for example, friends scattered all over the world. It takes time to make a friendship. These friends are too much scattered. There are men and women very dear to me whose minds I admire, whose characters I admire, that I would like to see often, that I do not see once in two years. Of what use are such friends, after all? I get up from my desk here, where I have been at work, bending over my typewriter for several hours. I would like to go walk now. I have certain problems concerned with my own work I would like to talk over with others. I think of Paul, Maurice, Tom, Fred, Kate, Will. These are all people interested in what interests me. Where are they?

They are scattered over the wide world. At least, if I make any friends here, in my own Virginia county, I can put my hands on them. We can go fishing or swimming. We can take a walk together under the trees in the evening. In the country this happens:

even the country roads you travel, often the streams you fish, the strips of woods in which you walk become presently as friends.

In that spot, on a certain country road in Smyth County, a certain thing I had tried for a year to get straight in my head suddenly got itself pretty straight. I remember that. It was a good feeling. I remember it every time I pass the spot. I remember where certain wild flowers always appear in this county in the spring, where certain bass lie in the streams, how certain hills look in the evening light, how nice some of the farmhouses are, as seen from the road as you drive past.

I have, as I have said, written certain things about the possibilities of country weeklies. It isn't just because they are country weeklies.

As I have said, a country weekly can easily enough be lazy and no-account.

Someone has just sent me such a weekly. It is here on my desk as I write. In this particular issue of this paper there are just 137 inches of live news and 25 inches of editorial matter. Then there are 8 inches of matter about sports. That's all. All the rest is canned stuff. Canned stuff is sent out from Chicago to weeklies like ours and sold to editors at $1.00 to $1.30 a page. It is got up by people who want to sell more pineapples, who want you to travel more on railroad trains, who want you to eat more of this or that or spend your money for this or that. They send it in all ready to drop into the paper. It doesn't cost a cent.

Or you can get comic strips pretty cheap. It is all easier than going out and getting the news of your county.

Well, our own papers are not all they should be. We aren't necessarily bragging but, during the same week the paper mentioned above was issued, we did publish 378 instead of 137 inches of live news and sixty-five instead of twenty-five inches of editorial matter.

We are all for the country weeklies and their possibilities but, as suggested above, a country weekly can also be, easily enough, as lazy and insipid and no-account as anything we know of in this world.

SORGHUM, CORN, AND APPLES

October 8

This is a rare time of the year to live in Marion and Smyth County. It is the time of apple-picking, the time of corn-cutting, of sorghum-making. There has been a lot of sorghum cane planted this year. C. F. Thomas, father of Emmett and Duke Thomas and proprietor of the Birch Spring Farm, out Shooting Creek way at the foot of the mountain, had out more than four acres.

C. F. Thomas is a particularly vigorous man. He is well into the seventies but that doesn't matter to him. He is cheerful and hard-working and an adventurous man, ready any time to do a hard day's work in the field with the best of them. He says he got gypped on tobacco last year; so he is giving sorghum a run this year.

The Thomas farm at the foot of Slemp Mountain is a delightful place. There are many small buildings out at the back of the main house. Old man Thomas is something of a mechanical genius. There are in the small buildings back of his house all sorts of tools for making all sorts of things. You will find there belts, pulleys, and lathes; and a lot of Mr. Thomas' time is put in making things. Last year he was hard at work making a new invention for cutting corn. He was absorbed in it for weeks and having a grand time. I don't know how it came out.

He and his son, Duke, live alone in the house but there are always visitors dropping in. Just now his daughter, Mrs. T. P. Tudor of Cincinnati, is at home with her husband and there are children playing about the house.

The corn in the corn fields of Smyth County is being rapidly cut. In the valleys and on the hillsides it is standing everywhere in its shocks. It stands up like armies at attention. There are companies and battalions and regiments of corn. It is like an army standing at attention in the fields. There the army stands prepared to fight on man's side in the grim battle against want.

There will be want and hunger in the cities this winter. There should be none here. General Lee's army in the last desperate months before the surrender lived almost entirely upon corn. We will have plenty of corn and apples. We will have cabbage. We'll eat.

There are three men sitting on a fall night on the courthouse steps in Marion, Virginia. Their talk is all of the fields and the crops. Men have gathered together on fall evenings and talked of the same thing for thousands of years. In this group are Sam Dillard, Will Hopkins, and Jim Arney.

They are talking about apples, corn, sorghum, cabbage, and the wheat planting. Jim Arney has at least a thousand bushels of apples on his trees. "I'm going to make a lot of cider," he says. He may make fifty barrels of cider and sell his apples in that way. The apple crop in Smyth County this year is immense. All over Smyth County grape vines hang heavy with grapes.

Sam Dillard is planting wheat. Will Hopkins will plant wheat on his farm next week.

There is something amazing and fine in the way American farmers go on year after year. Crops will not bring much money this year. There is little question but that, in the distribution of favors by the government, capital, as represented by the big manufacturers and by the banks, has got it all. When there are any favors handed out, they are handed to the industrialists. They have been nursed and coddled like babes while the farmer and factory workers have pretty much got it in the neck.

It doesn't stop the farmer. He goes on. Labor in America is touchingly grateful for anything done for labor. There is patience, a determination in the average man that stirs the soul.

Sam Dillard says, "I won't have hardly any nubbins to throw to my cows this year. All the ears on my corn are big."

"Mine, too," says Will Hopkins.

"Mine, too," says Jim Arney.

"They are so big and heavy they fairly fall out of the husks of their own weight," Sam Dillard says.

"There has been little or no disease in the corn this year. The ears are all heavy."

It is good to go for a visit to Love Bonham's apple-sorting shed south of Chilhowie just now. The pickers, men and women, are at work in the Bonham orchards and the sorters and packers are at work in the sorting shed. In the Bonham sorting shed you will see the finest and best apples in this whole section. You will see them being carefully picked and carefully sorted. They will be put away in cold storage, each apple carefully wrapped. Love Bonham is an intelligent and progressive orchardist, one of the best in the state. It is good to see any man doing his job well.

It is good to see the sorghum being made. Up Shooting Creek way lives Walter Pugh, formerly of Grayson County . . . and now he is making sorghum. He hasn't so much cane and is pressing it out in the old-fashioned way. A horse walks in a circle pressing the cane. It will be boiled in the old-fashioned way. By the time this is printed his sorghum will be made.

At the C. F. Thomas place they have got an elaborate arrangement for the sorghum-making. The cane-presser there is run by a gasoline engine. The juice from the cane flows through a pipe into a barrel and then into the boiler.

The boiler is of a new sort. The juice flows across it, slowly, up and down, up and down. It travels slowly across the long boiler and as it flows it is being skimmed by women who are experts at the job. Mr. and Mrs. Dixon, who live on the Thomas farm, and Mrs. Cora Tilson are doing the experting.

There is a sweet smell arising. In the daytime the bees from distant hives come on a visit.

Visitors come. Neighbors come. The boiling starts at dawn and goes on until night. Mr. Thomas is putting his sorghum up in glass jars, neatly labeled. It is good stuff. It will be shipped here and there.

The harvest moon is waning now. Nights are getting colder. Cider-making, apple-picking, corn-cutting, wheat-planting, syrup-making, frost in the air.

Fall. A good fall in this section. At least this section of mountain and valley country can face the coming winter without the fear that now lies like lead on the minds of city workers. No matter what happens in the industrial world the people in this section should eat. They should eat well. There is plenty of it.

TRAVEL NOTES

November 19

I am going about to colleges speaking, having two subjects on which I speak—machinery and newspapers. I am talking about the difference between the big city daily and the little country weekly such as I own in Marion. I am in the East now, but later, in January, I shall go into the Middle West and, in the early spring, to the Pacific coast. I am going mostly to colleges and universities, but in some places I speak also before men's clubs.

A manager in New York arranges all of this for me. In my contract with him there is a change. "No women's clubs," it says. This is not because I have any prejudice against women's clubs. Usually, they are culture-seeking clubs. I do not see how they are going to get any culture from me. Besides, I am talking and thinking on subjects not perhaps especially interesting to women.

For a long time now I have been especially interested in factories. For two or three winters, when I have been away from Marion, I have been spending a large part of my time going to factories and studying them. It seems to me that the men and women of our day, and especially the young men and women, are coming into a new world, essentially different from the world into which I came as a young man.

I am writing this in a hotel in the midst of a great industrial district near Pittsburgh. It is as different from our own Smyth County world as the country of Thomas Jefferson was different from the world of President Hoover. In my study of factories I have found everywhere machinery becoming more and more automatic, and that means that all the time more and more goods are being made with fewer men employed. The man not employed cannot buy goods. You have, you see, a vicious circle that may very well grow worse instead of better.

For example, I am told that we have now, in this country, machinery to make twenty pairs of shoes every year for every man, woman, and child in America.

This is only one case. . . . Most industries are becoming like that. Formerly we could ship all of our excess goods abroad but now, in all of our big markets—South America, India, etc.—machinery is being set up. Russia was formerly a great market. Now Russia has begun to pour goods out into the world.

And then also the position of the worker in the modern, high-speed factories has changed. His work has also become more and more automatic, less interesting. All the time it requires of the workers less and less skill. This, it seems to me, is doing something to the worker, making him perhaps less manly. I think the quality of a man's manhood depends a good deal upon his work.

Too, I think this whole question is of tremendous importance, particularly to young men and women. Some of these days it will have to be met by the government. Surely it is not very sound, when men are thrown out of work for no cause with which they have anything to do, to meet the situations by making pensioners of them, putting them on charity. That is degrading to a man, too.

Why, for all of this, I haven't any definite solutions, but in going about like this I have many opportunities to discuss it with students, manufacturers, economists. They all seem to think, as I do, that before long the government will have to begin to discuss it. We will all have to be thinking of it and trying to find a solution.

It may be that the Communists can work out a solution but there are a lot of dangers in that, too. There is the danger that the government may make life unbearable, too, by crushing out all individualism.

And the Communists also have to try to solve the many problems. It is simply an exchange of one kind of goods for another. Money must be handled, and when money is handled, the shrewd man will probably get it.

But, just the same, the problem brought into the world by modern high-speed machinery has to be met. The whole quality of our civilization in America in the future may well depend upon our brains and courage in trying to meet it.

And then I am also talking on newspapers. There is a tremendous interest in this subject, particularly in universities where they have schools of journalism. I am trying to interest bright, talented young men and women in going into the country weekly field. There is, I believe, a tremendous opportunity in our country weeklies. There isn't any reason why the best brains of the country shouldn't go into the country weekly.

Not because there is any money in it; there isn't. If a man makes a living it's enough. But there is an opportunity to improve printing and to make the local weeklies of great importance to the communities in which they are published. I find, as I go about talking on this subject, that more and more of the talented young men and women in the schools and universities are thinking less and less of how much money they can make and more about finding a life of more satisfying, individualistic work.

"I am a man who has tried to escape. It has been a game. Publishing a newspaper has been but one turn of the game I have tried to play with life. . . . Tomorrow I may try something else,"[1] Sherwood Anderson wrote in the summer of 1929 for readers of his country newspapers. He had refused late in 1928 even to consider selling the *Smyth County News* and the *Marion Democrat,* but just over a month later his mood was one of frustration:

> Everything of my routine of life has been disturbed for a long time now. I have been trying to work, but have not got much done. It is very interesting and absorbing running the country weeklies during the last year—but they have taken a lot of time.
> Now my son Bob, who is twenty-one, is with me and will be able to do a lot of the work. I hope to be able to get free from so many of the details that had piled up on me and that I shall have a book or two in the next year.[2]

1. "Response," *Smyth County News,* July 18, 1929, p. 1.
2. Letter to Gertrude Stein, January 15, 1929.

Obviously, Anderson had come to think of his newspapers as impediments to his career. Although he had found much happiness in writing and publishing them, he faced another crisis of despair, arising from dissatisfaction with always living in a small town, strained marital relations, concern over the welfare of his children, and the desire to write fiction again.

Sherwood Anderson and his third wife had worked together in 1928 to publish the *Marion Democrat* and the *Smyth County News*. She had managed the business and correspondence for the printshop; and Sherwood had gathered news, written articles, and enjoyed his freedom to rove about Marion and Smyth County. Soon after his wife decided that he was too difficult to live with, Anderson wrote: "It has been a bad year for me in many ways. The papers here are going off successfully and we have more than met our schedule as far as they are concerned, but my personal life has been rather a wreck. I have been married three times and evidently cannot make a success of marriage. My last marriage has fallen to pieces during the last eight months. This has hurt me a good deal more than anyone has known. To try in the midst of it to run the newspapers here successfully and to keep some hold on my real work at the same time has kept me in a distraught, upset state." [3]

When Sherwood Anderson was asked publicly why he had given up his newspapers he always said that he had been "forced" out of the printshop by his son, Robert Lane Anderson, who, after attending the University of Virginia and working as a reporter in Philadelphia, came to Marion early in 1929 to run the *News* and the *Democrat* for his father. Making Robert Anderson editor of the newspapers [4] was at once a convenient excuse for Sherwood to be out of Marion and a way to help the young man find work. When he sold control of the two papers to Robert in December, 1931, Sherwood Anderson gave the proceeds to his two older children, John and Marion. For the rest of his life, Anderson tried to help the three children whom he had deserted in 1913.

In 1929 Anderson wrote to Burton Emmett, who had helped him

3. Letter to Burton Emmett, March 10, 1929.
4. Robert Lane Anderson continued to publish the *Marion Democrat* and the *Smyth County News*, combined into the *Smyth County News* in 1941, until his death in 1951. The only extant files of the newspapers edited by Sherwood Anderson are in the printshop in Marion, Virginia.

initiate his newspaper venture in 1927, "I was in a desperate situation, not necessarily financially but for something definite to do that would carry me through this distraught time. If it is any satisfaction to you I think I can say to you that owning these papers has perhaps saved me from insanity." [5] But now that the newspapers had fulfilled their original purpose, Anderson hoped that returning to writing for his living would lead him from the new depth of hopelessness, as editing the newspapers had helped in the last crisis.

Publishing the *Smyth County News* and the *Marion Democrat* was indeed an agreeable and useful pastime to Sherwood Anderson, but the newspaper work had great influence on a surprising amount of the material that he wrote after abandoning the Marion printshop. In fact, almost all of the writer's published work after 1930 is a form of sophisticated journalism.

In 1929 Sherwood Anderson became acquainted with Miss Eleanor Copenhaver, an attractive, cultured member of one of Marion's oldest and most respected families. Miss Copenhaver was Industrial Secretary of the Young Women's Christian Association, and her duties included traveling widely to examine the working conditions of laborers in the factories that were beginning to feel the movement for full union organization. Anderson began to accompany Miss Copenhaver, whom he married in 1933, in order to observe the strikes and demonstrations that often erupted violently in factory towns. From these experiences Sherwood Anderson wrote such articles as "Cotton Mill," [6] "Danville, Virginia," [7] "Factory Town," [8] "I Want to Work," [9] and "Mill Girls." [10] In these articles and in the novel *Beyond Desire*,[11] Anderson reported to the public the atrocities of the industrial system of modern America and revealed his sympathy for the working classes.

As were so many Americans in the early 1930's, Sherwood Anderson was temporarily attracted to communism as a possible solu-

5. Letter of March 10, 1929.
6. *Scribner's Magazine*, LXXXVIII (July, 1930), 1–11.
7. *New Republic*, LXV (January 21, 1931), 266–68.
8. *Ibid.*, LXII (March 26, 1930), 143–44.
9. *Today*, I (April 28, 1934), 10–12, 22.
10. *Scribner's Magazine*, XCI (January, 1932), 8–12, 59–64.
11. New York: Liveright, Inc., 1932.

tion to the unsolved problems of the Great Depression. Anderson
wrote of the communist movement sympathetically in such articles
as "Let's Have More Criminal Syndicalism," [12] "Listen, Mr. President," [13] "The Price of Aristocracy," [14] and "How I Came to Communism." [15] Anderson may have believed himself to be a communist, but even in "How I Came to Communism" there is an em-
phatic comment by him on the role of the writer in the communist
movement: "I believe and am bound to believe that those of you
who are revolutionists will get the most help out of such men as
myself not by trying to utilize such talents as we have directly as
writers of propaganda but in leaving us as free as possible to strike,
by our stories out of American life, into the deeper facts." [16]

Besides his campaigns for country journalism and labor organization, Anderson wrote many reports on his experiences among the
Virginia mountain people. He loved the distant tenderness and the
fierce independence of the men and women he had come to know
in Southwest Virginia, and he wrote of their lives in "City Gangs
Enslave Moonshine Mountaineers," [17] "Jug of Moon," [18] "A Mountain Marriage," [19] "Virginia Justice," [20] and "A New Chance for the
Men of the Hills." [21] Anderson's last novel, *Kit Brandon,*[22] was the
story of a rum-runner from the Blue Ridge Mountains, based
directly on newspaper stories he had written in 1928. The last book
which Sherwood Anderson lived to publish, *Home Town,*[23] was a
testament to the love which the writer had in truth always felt for
the American small town. Illustrated with pictures from villages
across the nation, the book extolled not the virtues but the realities
of a disappearing way of life in the American village and town.

In Southwest Virginia Sherwood Anderson found at last not only

12. *New Masses,* VII (February, 1932), 3–6.
13. *Nation,* CXXXV (August 31, 1932), 191–93.
14. *Today,* I (March 10, 1934), 10–11, 23.
15. *New Masses,* VIII (September, 1932), 8–9.
16. *Ibid.,* p. 8.
17. *Liberty,* XII (November 2, 1935), 12–13.
18. *Today,* II (September, 1934), 6–7.
19. *Fight Against War and Fascism,* III (October, 1936), 16–17, 22–23.
20. *Today,* II (July 21, 1934), 6–7, 24.
21. *Today,* I (May 12, 1934), 10–11, 22–23.
22. New York: Charles Scribner's Sons, 1936. See Ray Lewis White, "The
Original for Sherwood Anderson's *Kit Brandon,*" *Newberry Library Bulletin,* VI
(December, 1965), 196–99.
23. New York: Alliance Book Corporation, 1940.

a home and work that was satisfying but also a wife who helped him achieve the happiness that had been always elusive in three previous marriages. From his marriage to Eleanor Copenhaver in 1933 until his death in 1941, Sherwood Anderson was for the first time happy with his wife, his past work, and whatever present task he set himself. The old periods of despair never completely disappeared, but Anderson's despair over them mellowed and softened into an acceptance of whatever joy and fame were granted to him.

Sherwood Anderson's career as a Virginia newspaper editor was indeed "an episode unique in American newspaper history, the first time a mature writer has been completely responsible for the contents of two country papers." [24] But this is much less important than the fact that writing and publishing two such newspapers was an important part of the life of the author who wrote for use on his gravestone that now overlooks Marion, Virginia: "Life Not Death Is the Great Adventure."

24. James Schevill, *Sherwood Anderson: His Life and Work* (Denver: University of Denver Press, 1951), p. 247.

A NOTE ON EDITING

Preparing a sampler of Sherwood Anderson's country newspaper columns has entailed three problems: attribution, selection, and textual procedure. I must briefly explain my handling of these problems in compiling this book.

First, not every item that appeared in the *Smyth County News* and the *Marion Democrat* between the first of November, 1927, and the last of December, 1931, was written by Sherwood Anderson. Anderson frequently printed letters, news releases, and prepared copy without indicating that the writing was not his own. Such material, readily distinguishable to an Anderson devotee, I have omitted from this volume, along with signed contributed material.

The major attributive difficulty arises from the presence of columns written by Robert Lane Anderson, who began contributing to his father's papers in January, 1929, and who was soon writing most of the material published. Robert Lane Anderson showed a remarkable ability to imitate Sherwood Anderson's journalistic style. As the son assumed a public identity similar to his father's in Marion and Smyth County, he adopted his father's friends, his interests, and even his Buck Fever creation. When Sherwood Anderson left Virginia for sometimes weeks of travel, Robert Anderson maintained the whimsical storyteller's tone and the mythical creations of his father's writing. To generalize, Robert Anderson's writing at its best is indistinguishable from Sherwood's at its most rushed and careless moments. (There could never, therefore, be an authoritative collection of *all* items signed "Buck Fever.") So that I may err, if at all, in the direction of caution, I have chosen to collect only those later (usually post-1928) items that are signed by Sherwood Anderson or that appear in his personal columns—"What Say!" and "A Traveler's Notes."

The second and more difficult problem is that of selecting from several hundred enjoyable newspaper stories written by Sherwood Anderson the relative few that can appear in my sampler. I have guided my choice by establishing three areas of interest: (1) Anderson's own comments on his venture into country journalism, (2) news items at once typical of Anderson's newspaper style and demonstrative of his fascinatingly bittersweet attitude toward small-town life, and (3) personal essays that range from Anderson's autobiographical reminiscences to expressions of love for his adopted Southwest Virginia to manifestations of his concern over America's political condition in the early 1930's. By selecting from four years instead of twelve months of Anderson's newspaper writing, I have necessarily lost some of the continuity and the seasonal intensity that obtain in *Hello Towns!* Yet thereby does my collection, I believe, do more justice to Sherwood Anderson's career from the buying of his papers in 1927 to his assigning them to Robert Lane Anderson at the end of 1931.

Finally, the existence of *Hello Towns!* could have complicated my textual problems. However, the newspaper items that constitute *Hello Towns!* are not printed therein exactly as they appeared in the *Smyth County News* and the *Marion Democrat*. Examination of the columns mounted for *Hello Towns!*, now in The Newberry Library's Sherwood Anderson Collection, reveals that Anderson severely edited his stories for publication in book form. There are pervasive changes in wording, punctuation, spelling, and even dating. I have, therefore, dispensed wholly with *Hello Towns!* except for incorporating into my text infrequent obvious corrections (as in proper names) which Anderson made in editing news stories for his book. I have not let publication in *Hello Towns!* influence my choice of stories for this volume. I have, however, omitted items that enjoyed simultaneous publication in Anderson's newspapers and in periodicals.

In presenting Sherwood Anderson's country news stories as exactly as possible as they first appeared, I have leaned heavily on one fact: Anderson could never have carefully proofread his articles after they were linotyped for the presses. Considering this, in addition to the always rushed and usually hectic conditions of a country newspaper office and Anderson's cavalier dismissal of the importance of punctuation in first drafts, I have regularized all punctuation and spelling and unobtrusively corrected a few errors in such basic forms as subject-verb agreement. Because the same news stories appeared in the *Smyth County News* and the *Marion Democrat* I have, unless otherwise noted, taken my samples from the *Smyth County News*. The extent of annotation is governed by the fact that my book is primarily a "reader," not a "text."

A SELECTED BIBLIOGRAPHY

This checklist is exhaustive only in listing books by and about Sherwood Anderson. Those books that contain material especially valuable to the study of Anderson's newspaper career are marked with an asterisk. The lists of unpublished manuscripts and typescripts available at The Newberry Library are presented as a convenient guide to the relevant Sherwood Anderson Papers, which are well catalogued but not yet indexed. The bibliography compiled by Sheehy and Lohf lists most of the articles and essays by and about Sherwood Anderson as well as the nearly thirty theses and dissertations completed through 1959. The Sullivan thesis is recommended as a useful, workmanlike survey of Sherwood Anderson's ideas about country journalism. The Reser thesis is both superficial and carelessly written.

I. WORKS BY SHERWOOD ANDERSON

A. *Books*

> *Windy McPherson's Son.* New York: John Lane Company, 1916; New York: B. W. Huebsch, 1922 (revised); Chicago: University of Chicago Press, 1965.

Marching Men. New York: John Lane Company, 1917.

Mid-American Chants. New York: John Lane Company, 1918.

Winesburg, Ohio. New York: B. W. Huebsch, 1919; New York: Modern Library [1919]; New York: Viking Press, 1960 [with critical essays, edited by John H. Ferres, 1966].

Poor White. New York: B. W. Huebsch, 1920. New York: Viking Press, 1966.

The Triumph of the Egg. New York: B. W. Huebsch, 1921.

Horses and Men. New York: B. W. Huebsch, 1923.

Many Marriages. New York: B. W. Huebsch, 1923.

A Story Teller's Story. New York: B. W. Huebsch, 1924; New York: Grove Press, 1958.

Dark Laughter. New York: Boni and Liveright, 1925, 1960.

The Modern Writer. San Francisco: Lantern Press, 1925.

*Sherwood Anderson's Notebook. New York: Boni and Liveright, 1926.

Tar: A Midwest Childhood. New York: Boni and Liveright, 1926.

A New Testament. New York: Boni and Liveright, 1926.

Alice and The Lost Novel. London: Elkin Mathews and Marrot, 1929.

*Hello Towns! New York: Horace Liveright, 1929.

*Nearer the Grass Roots. San Francisco: Westgate Press, 1929.

The American County Fair. New York: Random House, 1930.

Perhaps Women. New York: Horace Liveright, 1932.

Beyond Desire. New York: Liveright, Inc., 1932, 1961.

Death in the Woods. New York: Liveright, Inc., 1933.

No Swank. Philadelphia: Centaur Press, 1934.

Puzzled America. New York: Charles Scribner's Sons, 1935.

Kit Brandon. New York: Charles Scribner's Sons, 1936.

Plays, Winesburg and Others. New York: Charles Scribner's Sons, 1937.

A Writer's Conception of Realism. Olivet, Michigan: Olivet College, 1939.

Five Poems. San Mateo, California: Quercus Press, 1939.

*Home Town. New York: Alliance Book Corporation, 1940.

*Sherwood Anderson's Memoirs. New York: Harcourt, Brace and Company, 1942.

*The Sherwood Anderson Reader, edited by Paul Rosenfeld. New York: Houghton Mifflin Company, 1947.

The Portable Sherwood Anderson, edited by Horace Gregory. New York: Viking Press, 1949.
Letters of Sherwood Anderson, edited by Howard Mumford Jones and Walter B. Rideout. Boston: Little, Brown and Company, 1953.
Sherwood Anderson: Short Stories, edited by Maxwell Geismar. New York: Hill and Wang, 1962.

B. *Articles*

"The Country Weekly," *Forum,* LXXXV (April, 1931), 208–13.
"I Will Not Sell My Papers," *Outlook,* CL (December 5, 1928), 1286–87.
"On Being a Country Editor," *Vanity Fair,* XXIX (February, 1928), 70, 92.
"Small Town Notes," *Vanity Fair,* XXX (June, 1928), 58, 120; XXXII (April, 1929), 72, 106; XXXII (July, 1929), 48, 110; XXXIII (September, 1929), 72, 110, 114.
"The Small Town Paper," Preface to Robert Lane Anderson's *Thwarted Ambitions* (Marion, Virginia: Marion Publishing Company, n.d.), n.p.

C. *Manuscripts*

"Address to the State Meeting of Newspaper Men at Athens, Georgia."
"The American Small Town: Meet the Editor."
"The City Daily: The Harris Lectures, Number I, Northwestern University."
"The Country Weekly: The Harris Lectures, Number II, Northwestern University."
"How I Ran a Small Town Newspaper."
"Journalism."
"Journalism and the Young Writer."
"Newspapers: A Speech Delivered at the Institute of Public Affairs at the University of Virginia," in MS "Book of Days."
"On Being a Country Editor."
"Review of Henry Beetle Hough's *Country Editor.*"
Letters to:
  Alexander, Will W. January 3, 1931.
  Anderson, Cornelia Lane. February 21, 1929.

Anderson, John. [October, 1927]; [1928].
Anderson, Karl. [Fall, 1927]; March 3, 1928; [January, 1932].
Bockler, Charles. [Early 1929].
Burrow, Trigant. January 12, 1928.
Emmett, Burton. [October, 1927]; October 24, 1927; [December, 1927]; [Spring, 1928]; December 6, 1928; December 21, 1928; February 21, 1929; March 10, 1929.
Koskull, Baroness Marie. [Early 1929].
Liveright, Horace. February 21, 1929.
Loos, Anita. [1928].
Morrow, Marco. [November, 1927].
Risley, Edward. December 6, 1937.
Schevill, Ferdinand. March 3, 1928.
Stein, Gertrude. [Winter, 1927]; [December, 1927]; [1928]; January 15, 1929.
Stieglitz, Alfred. October 10, 1927; [December, 1927]; March 28, 1928.

II. WORKS ABOUT SHERWOOD ANDERSON

A. Books

*Anderson, David. *Sherwood Anderson*. New York: Holt, Rinehart and Winston, 1967.
Burbank, Rex. *Sherwood Anderson*. New York: Twayne Publishers, 1964.
Chase, Cleveland B. *Sherwood Anderson*. New York: R. M. McBride, 1927.
Fagin, Nathan Bryllion. *The Phenomenon of Sherwood Anderson: A Study in American Life and Letters*. Baltimore: Rossi-Bryn, 1927.
*Howe, Irving. *Sherwood Anderson*. New York: William Sloane, 1951; Stanford: Stanford University Press, 1966.
The Newberry Library Bulletin, 2d Ser., No. 2 (December, 1948). The Sherwood Anderson Memorial Number.
*Schevill, James. *Sherwood Anderson: His Life and Work*. Denver: University of Denver Press, 1951.
*Sheehy, Eugene P. and Kenneth A. Lohf. *Sherwood Anderson: A Bibliography*. Los Gatos, California: Talisman Press, 1960.
Shenandoah, XIII (Spring, 1962). The Sherwood Anderson Issue.

Story, XXIX (September–October, 1941). The Sherwood Anderson Memorial Number.

Sutton, William A. *Exit to Elsinore*. Muncie, Indiana: Ball State University, 1967.

Weber, Brom. *Sherwood Anderson*. Minneapolis: University of Minnesota Press, 1964.

*White, Ray Lewis, editor. *The Achievement of Sherwood Anderson: Essays in Criticism*. Chapel Hill: University of North Carolina Press, 1966.

B. *Articles*

Adams, Mildred. "A Small-Town Editor Airs His Mind," *New York Times Magazine*, December 22, 1929, pp. 3, 20.

"Back to Ole Virginny," *New York Times*, November 20, 1927, III, p. 4.

Brooks, Walter R. "Picked at Random," *Outlook*, CLII (May 8, 1929), 78.

Buchanan, Annabel Morris. "Sherwood Anderson: Country Editor," *World Today*, LIII (February, 1929), 249–53.

Dickinson, L. R. "Smyth County Items," *Outlook*, CXLVIII (April 11, 1928), 581–83.

"Editor Anderson at Play," *New York Times*, August 29, 1928, V, p. 20.

Gannett, Lewis. "The Cracker Box Philosopher," *New York Herald Tribune Books*, May 5, 1929, p. 3.

Geismar, Maxwell. "Sherwood Anderson: Last of the Townsmen," *The Last of the Provincials: The American Novel, 1915–1925* (Boston: Houghton Mifflin Company, 1947), pp. 219–84.

Haardt, Sara. "Hello Towns," *Saturday Review of Literature*, V (May 4, 1929), 974.

Hellman, Geoffrey T. "Hello, Sherwood," *New Republic*, LVIII (May 15, 1929), 365.

Lovett, Robert Morss. "Sherwood Anderson," *New Republic*, LXXXIX (November 25, 1936), 103–5.

Mallory, Rose. "The Celebrity in Our Town," *New York Herald Tribune Sunday Magazine*, July 2, 1928, n.p.

Mencken, H. L. "Experiments by Old Hands," *American Mercury*, XVII (June, 1929), 253–54.

Moley, Raymond. Editor's note in *Today*, I (December 2, 1933), 3.

"Novelist Buys Papers," *New York Times,* October 19, 1927, IV, p. 10.

Rideout, Walter B. "Why Sherwood Anderson Employed Buck Fever," *Georgia Review,* XIII (Spring, 1959), 76–85. Reprinted in White, *The Achievement of Sherwood Anderson,* pp. 128–37.

"Son Buys Sherwood Anderson Out," *New York Times,* January 1, 1932, p. 30.

"Suburban Weeklies," *New York Times,* May 2, 1929, p. 26.

"Triumph of the Egg," *New York Times,* October 23, 1927, III, p. 4.

White, Ray Lewis. "The Original for Sherwood Anderson's *Kit Brandon,*" *Newberry Library Bulletin,* VI (December, 1965), 196–99.

White, William Allen. "The Country Editor Speaks," *Nation,* CXXVIII (June 12, 1929), 714.

C. *Theses*

Reser, James A. "Sherwood Anderson: Country Newspaper Editor-Owner-Publisher," East Tennessee State University, 1964.

Sullivan, John H. "Sherwood Anderson's Idea of the Country Weekly Newspaper," Marquette University, 1960.

D. *Manuscripts*

Letters from:
  Alexander, Will W. December 31, 1930.
  Canby, Henry Seidel. November 18, 1927.
  Del Vecchio, Thomas. January 30, 1928.
  Gale, A. L. December 7, 1927.
  Haggerty, James. November 29, 1927.
  Hurd, Herman, Jr. July 30, 1934.
  Liveright, Ida. September 10, 1928.
  Loos, Anita. November 28, 1927.
  Piercy, Josephine. December 7, 1928.
  Porterfield, Robert. March 13, 1941.
  Prows, Harry J. June 9, 1935.
  Putzel, Max. January 25, 1939.
  Sackett, Sheldon F. April 1, 1931.
  Sagmaster, Howard. April 6, 1931.
  Schevill, Ferdinand. November 13, 1927.

Shipman, Don. September 30, 1937.
Smith, William S. August 5, 1934.
Stieglitz, Alfred. January 7, 1928.
Stryker, Howard. January 1, 1938.
Wead, Robert. March 16, 1931.
Whelan, Ken. February 5, 1935.
Wolinsky, Paul. April 7, 1930.

www.ingramcontent.com/pod-product-compliance
Lightning Source LLC
Chambersburg PA
CBHW020348270326
41926CB00007B/343